Islam,
Civil Society &
Market Economy

Ahmet Aslan

Norman Barry

Detmar Doering

Mustafa Erdoğan

Chandran Kukathas

Atilla Yayla (ed.)

LIBERTE BOOKS

Liberte Books: 30
ISBN 975-6877-15-4

Islam, Civil Society and Market Economy

© Association for Liberal Thinking
First Print: 1999

Editor
Atilla YAYLA

Cover
Levent Korkut

Preperation for Print
Siyasal Typing House

Printed by
Yardımcı-Ofset Printing Ltd. Co.
(0.312) 342 26 27

It was published by Liberte Books for
the Association for Liberal Thinking

Liberte Books
GMK Bulvarı No:108/17 06570 Maltepe-Ankara-Turkey
Tel: 312/230 37 19 Faks: 312/230 80 03
e-mail: liberal@ada.net.tr Web: liberal-dt.org.tr

CONTENT

INTRODUCTION: ISLAM OR DEMOCRACY?

Atilla Yayla[*]

Ten years ago there were twenty democratic countries all over the world. Democracy used to appear as a regime confined to the countries in West Europe and North America. In other parts of the world anti-democratic regimes dominated for decades in the form of authoritarianism or totalitarianism. Indeed, a large part of world fell under ideologically sophisticated socialist regimes while the rest was in essence under the control of brute left or right wing authorianism.

There was a sharp difference between the two kinds of anti-democratic regimes. Authorian systems did not pretend to be democratic in any sense. In contrast socialist countries attempted to redefine the word democracy to have a ground on which to claim that they are the real or more progressive democracies. Thus they called themselves "people's democracy" that meant in practise suppression of the people by a tiny minority gathered in the single-party apparatus. This caused blurring in the meaning of democracy that lasted for quite a long time.

Towards the end of 1980s a rapid change swept all over the world. Totalitarian regimes of socialism started falling down one by one. The first move happened in central European Countries which was followed by East European socialist regimes. The collapse and disintegration of the Soviet Union marked the final triumph of democracy over socialist totalitarianism. This was named as "white revolution" which was the starting point of what Samuel Huntington called as "the third wave of democracy." This also helped accelerate democratization process in undemocratic

[*] *Professor of Political Theory and Political Economy, Hacettepe University, Ankara, Turkey.*

countries. Thus ruling elites in many countries were ousted sometimes peacefully and in other cases by force. The overall result was rapid spread of democracy in all continents. Indeed more than 110 countries today claim to be democratic or trying to democratize themselves.

However there is an exception to this general phenomenon. We have a large region where third ware of democracy, like the previous ones, seem to have no serious influence: the Middle East. Indeed, in the Middle East, which is mainly home to Muslim countries, democratic regime is really an exception. For long time only two countries, Turkey and Israel, have been considered to have reasonably well-functioning democracies. This may be no longer so. In recent years Turkey went under a process in which basic rights and freedoms of large masses were brutely suppressed by state elites in the name of "modernism", "secularism" and even democracy. Turkey lost the sense of rule of law, inviolable human rights, and secularism which is a tool of social peace and state's impartiality with respect to religious stances. Turkey has now a unique regime which mixes different aspects to democracy, authoritarianism and totalitarianism.

On no accounts are any one of other Islamic countries in a better position than Turkey in this respect. In some Islamic countries, like Syria, Iraq, and to a certain extent Egypt, we see dictatorships that differ from each other only in the degree of brutalism. In some others monarchies-dynasties with no respect to basic human rights and rule of law reign like Saudia Arabia and small Golf countries. Then there are those regimes in North Africa which have desperately been trying to modernize or to secularize their country at the expense of human rights, and rule of law. In none of Islamic countries, including Turkey, the ruling elites really want their people to have a real say in public affairs. Some regularly hold elections not as a tool of power sharing peacefully but rather as a show to impress outsiders and to crack down actual and potential opponents.

Why is this so? Why do not we see real democracies in Islamic countries. This is a question for whose answer those who live in these countries should spend brain-power, time, and energy at least as much as Western observers. The question can be tackled at two levels, the first being practical and the second theoretical. There are many reasons to be pessimistic on practial level. As mentioned above, Islamic countries neither wish their people to have a say in conducting public affairs nor they respect human rights. In all Islamic countries decision making is over-centralized, power sharing tools and mechanisms are very few, civil society tradition is extremely weak, and spontaneous forces of society are strictly obsctacled.

Does this mean that Islam is inherently incompatible with democracy? That question brings us to the second and theoretical level of analysis. We see here two main brands of thought: The first one pessimistic, and the second optimistic. I must emphasize at the outset that five authors whose articles included here are quite optimistic. I would like to hope that their optimism does not amounts to imagination. Let us have a look at what they thought of the subject before we proceed to evelute their position.

Norman Barry starts with a historical and intellectual account of civil society concept. That is followed by an analysis of the term. To him "the most important element" of civil society is "the rejection of centralised political arrangements which embody the features of Hobbesian sovereignty". That includes, of course, not only the limitation of executive branch of political power but also, and probably most importantly, of the legislature. To put it more openly, "the legislature should be limited by law not of its own making". Prof. Barry points out that the tools with which this can be achieved are a written constitution or common law. Thus the second important element of civil society comes out: rule of law. Because "only in conditions of liberty and the rule of law is there the possibility of the preservation and development of differing cultural arrangements, religious practises and moral traditions".

After underlining the importance of civil society, Barry moves to the relation between liberalism and religion. He draws our attention especially to the American case where despite a deep-rooted tradition of tolerance and religious freedom, problems arise from time to time. Barry calls the attitude of Federal Supreme Court in many cases as a kind of "liberal totalitarianism" which derives partly from "excessive legalism", and partly from growing intolerance against religious liberties in certain circles of the American society.

The centre point in Barry's article is "Islam, liberalism, and civil society". The author admits that at first glance Islam might seem uncomprising with either liberalism or civil society, especially when we look at social, cultural, and political structure in Islamic countries. However this may be misleading. The acts of "Muslim states that have done so much to discredit Islam" do not necessarily prove that Islam has nothing to do with civil society, rule of law, and market economy.

Despite the difficulties created by Islam's not having "one authoritative text that deals exclusively with forms of government", one can find some elements stimulative for rule of law and civil society. The first is the character of Islamic law. It binds not only believers but also the rulers. The sovereignty ends in God that means that there can be no absolute sovereign –be it a person or a group of persons. Barry says "there are.... no nation states" in Islamic teaching, Muslims are not divided by race or langugae. The law making process in Islamic traditions is also very interesting in his opinion. In Islam there is a Hayekian understanding of law making, that is, no concrete body has the final and absolute power to make law, it rather comes out from individual, uncoordinated reasoning of Muslim scholars.

In the last part of his article Prof. Barry mentions ethical imperatives in Islam like treating everbody equal, respecting humans including even enemies, caring for justice. He also traces features of pluralism in Islamic history. In his opinion, "Islam is closer to classical liberalism than it is to the egalitarian American variant". He also points out that "Islam can claim to have originated the theory of the free market a long time before Adam Smith..."

After pointing out so many positive points in Islam with respect to its relation with civil society and market economy, Barry raises a very important question: "Why has Islam not been recognised as part of mainstream liberal social and political theory since much of its doctrine is consisted with it?" I think this is the question for which especially Muslim liberals should seek a satisfactory answer. It is difficult not to share Barry's convincton that Muslim states acquired "quite the wrong doctrines from the West and many ideas which are alien to pure Islamic tradition". However, despite being a good starting point, this answer is not sufficiently explaining the problem in itself.

Chandran Kukathas searches the relationship between Islam, democracy and civil society in his article. He is quick in pointing out the groundlessness of the prejudices against Islam in the West. Starting his analysis with the concept of civil society, he first underlines the vagueness in the concept, and then goes on to mention historical roots of civil society. A main concern for him is the difference, if there is any, between society and civil society. In his understanding civil society could be seen as a "distinctively modern form of society."

The notion of civil society implies some ideas. The first is that "civil society means society as distinguished from the state." The second idea is freedom in the sense classical liberal philosophers defended. Kukathas strongly emphasizes that the idea of freedom embedded in civil society has nothing to do with the idea of freedom put forward by Karl Marx and J. Jack Rousseau. In Kukathas' view "the freedom embodied in civil society is the freedom that allows human beings to live together in spite of their differences and in spite of the conflicts which arise from their varying interests, temperament, and beliefs". It is this understanding of freedom that "makes civil society a notably modern idea." In its core lies the recognition of the fact that in all human societies "people worship different god, and this fact has to be accommodated by legal and political institutions if humans are to stand any chance of flourishing."

Like Barry, Kukathas does not ignore to touch upon the ties between civil society and market society: "Civil society is market society; but it is not just market society". I think this point deserves to be stressed again and again. On no account would it be an exaggeration to claim that a civil society without a market society will be something we can never have in this world. However, civil society does not only include business associations but also "associations to which people have attachments rooted less in their economic concerns than in their emotional attachments and moral commitments and so, in their identities. The most important associations or communities, here, are religious ones".

Moving from civil society concept to democracy Kukathas does express basic problem of democracy quite differently from conventional formulas. To him the problem is not who governs, but rather how to keep pluralism in society. As he puts, political problem "is no longer a problem of how to preserve unity; for such unity does no exist. It is a problem of how to make possible –and preserve- freedom: the freedom to live, and worship, differently". But this question is not easy to answer, "since differences here will not simply matters of taste but will raise questions about what is right, and how one should live". Kukathas mentions two kinds of solutions. The first is to settle the question of how one should live and then to impose it on all. The second is to leave the decision how to live to individuals and to provide a framework of meta-norms by which different ways could co-exist in peace and harmony. The first solution has no practical capacity to be applied as people disagree among themselves and resist again the imposition of beliefs upon themselves. It inevitable paves way for oppressive states. Thus, civil society has to turn to the second solution. It is at this point that the need for a more elaborated political theory appear. Kukathas is not shy to say that this political theory that tolerate the diversity of communities, associations, and traditions have been in existence for quite a long time and it is commonly labelled liberalism.

Having said that Kukathas raises another question: What is the place of religion in civil society? He points out that religion is still an important element of society despite the modernization and secularization: "We need to understand how the world has indeed become more secular; but we need also to appreciate why, and how, religion has an important place in modern civil society." In explaining why this is so, Kukathas uses a reasoning that reminds Humean and Hayekian thought. He tells us that reason alone can not guide human-beings in all aspects of life. Unaided reason fails especially about value or morality. If this is so, where we should turn to for appropriate answers. Kukathas counts again two possible sources: To look to nature and to apply to post-modernism. The first may not be successful enough as naturalism generates disagrement rather than consensus. The second seems worse as its offer bears no content and it, as Larmore said, "ends up confusing the rejection of philosophical rationalism with the abandonment of reason itself."

"If reason alone is not enough, and the extremes of naturalism and postmodernism offer no solution, upon what resources can we draw to address our fundamental concerns in matters of value?" asks Kukathas. How about tradition? The author is hopeful to find keys to the solution of this important question in tradition and places religion within his wide understandig of tradition. To Kukathas, religion has two important functions. "First it has been a source of substantive judgements on matters of value." Second, "religion.... has played an important role in constructing the undestandings which have socialised individuals." Therefore "the religion has a really important place in civil society", concludes Kukathas. This brings him closer to the more fundamental question of "what is, and should be, the political place of religion in civil society, and democratic civil society in particular."

Kukathas mentions two views about the place of religion in modern society both coming out of the European Enlishtenment. "The first suggests that religion ought to be repudiated as irrational." The second view is more moderate. It suggests that "religions should be recognized as something important to some people, and therefore tolerated within tightly defined limits." Kukathas himself is keen to reject both views because the first fails to understand the importance of religion in human society and the second falls away from a proper understanding of the nature of civil society.

He recognizes that religion can be a powerful and dangerous force in society. It attracs people and religious leaders who are able to mobilize large masses can have great power in their hands. It is tempting to use this power in their hands. It is also tempting to use this power in politics. However to use the power in hand is not peculiar to religious leaders, rather it is a general phenomenan. The real danger stems not from who has the power but rather from the concentration or usurpation of power. "If the alternative is to concentrate political authority in the hands of a power great enough to keep all, including religion, in awe, the cure might be worse than the potential disease." Indeed, as Kukathas rightly underlines, "the greatest tyrannies in this century were exerted by the godless states of communism, and by Germany under the influence of Nazi doctrines of religious hatred".

Like all liberals Kukathas favours the dispersion of power. "The greater the dispersal of power the better." Because each power holder "operates to constrain any one power from assuming a position of .... preeminence that tyranny becomes as possibility." Therefore it is good if there is a division of power between religion and state as long as none can take the upperhand.

There is not much doubt about this approach's validity with respect to christianity. However many scholars and politicians like to disclose the view that this does not hold for Islam, since they believe, Islam does not accept any separation between state and religious establishment. Kukathas does not think so. To him "Islam is not at adds with democracy or civil society", because it does not claim to embrace whole of society as long as there are unbelievers.

The author goes to historical examples, starting with the days of prophet Muhammed himself, to show how tolerant Islam has been against unbelievers and believers of other religions. He does not insist that "Islam's history is stainless". There had been times when tolerant disappeared and bloody conflicts happened. But this is true also for other religions. Islamic teaching has the capacity to be subject to tolerant interpretations. Therefore we should look to the "traditions which are ready to embrace norms of toleration."

Detmar Doering starts his article dealing with the subject at a more general level. He first summarizes a quite common view that "religion and civil society do not go well together." This is the view held in Europe since Voltaire. Conservatives criticized this view and said that religious truth could be reconciled with a secular concept of politics. Edmund Burke, for example, stressed that "man is religious animal" and without the support of religion no political system can survive long.

Doering finds some truth in both approaches. In his words, "Western civilisation and western civil society certainly owe much of its progress to some kind of secularism. On the other hand we see that the loss of social cohesion sometimes undermines even the most elementary rules of civil society." Then he attempts to solve the problem behind this conflict by looking at the meaning of "civil society."

In his opionion the most clear understanding of civil society comes from John Locke. Locke defines civil society as a political framework within which our lives, liberties, and estates are mutually preserved. Locke's theory does not need any religious assumption to function, though Locke tried to give a theological foundation to his theory. Locke's attempt to reconcile civil society with religion has not proved very successful, but nonetheless it helped eliminate some intolerant features of religion in practice.

Detmar Doering goes on analyising the relation between classical liberal conception of civil society and religion by comparing each's final aim. Religion is mainly concerned with end states. It does not aim to widen the choices before the person, rather it urges human beings to strictly follow its way. Liberalism offers to the individual an increase in the area of choice. Doering does not hesitate to say that "religion's concern for 'end states' can have positive consequences". But the view that a liberal civil society offers no concrete moral values to teach is in correct. Religion and other sources of values can live together to help make a civil society work smoothly.

Despite his tolerant approach to religion and religious values, Doering holds a secularist position and rejects some projudices about secularism stemming out of secularist and religious circles. He rejects government censure, but accepts that "there is a right to speak out about and to censure immoral tendencies in cultural life" while discussing about pornography. In his opinion, "liberty does not mean that nobody is allowed to tell you what you can or cannot do. Social ostracism and boycots are, although it may not always serve good purposes, legitimate means, to ensure that moral and religious standards have a voice in society." Another prejudice he rejects is that "a secularist state has to enforce secularist standards upon al social sub-structures of a civil society". Civil society implies peaceful society. It can not impose "its" views upon its citizens. The standard of civil society is not "levelling" secularism but "the possibility to pursue your own values within a framework of voluntary cooperation."

However Doering is aware of the fact that there are some prerequisities for civil society and religion to work together in peace: Communal structures that support religion should be "privatised." There must be a separation between religion, religious establishment and state. The members of religious communities must be free to organise themselves in an exclusive way. "Religious communities (like other special interest groups) must not instrumentalise government for their purposes, unless the purpose is the mere protection of their rights." Liberal secularism does not aim to secularize the private sphere but the politics.

He ends up by pointing out that to realize these requires "an enormous self-restraint- sometimes vitalised by constitutional mechanism- for both, religious and civil society itself." Otherwise, not only religion but also secularism might turn into threats to civil society. Indeed, is not he right when we bring any "secular" Islamic state under light?

The Turkish scholar Mustafa Erdoğan begins with a short account of developments in Turkish politics since 1995. It was a unique period for Turkey as for the first time in the history of Turkish Rebublic an Islamic oriented party, Welfare Party become the leading partner in a coalition government. As Erdoğan puts it, the secular establishment, the army being in its core, was not happy with this and it found out a way to force WP out of power. This provoked the ongoing debate about Islam's compatibility with democracy in general and Islam's place in Turkish politics in particular.

After that Erdoğan first turns to what he calls "a paradigmatic error" very common among Turkish scholars dealing with the subject. According to these scholars. Islam is an exceptional phenomenan in Turkish politics. It is even an outsider that has nothing to do with the sociological structure of the country. There can be no place for religion in modern, secular society. All Islamic appearces are "fundamentalist". The reasons for the rise of Islamic influence in social, political and economic life have been rapid urbanization, unbalanced modernization, "unfair" income distribution, and financial help or ideological manipulation from abroad.

However not all Turkish scholars adopt this approcah. There are some who see things in a different way. Among whom are Nilüfer Göle, Şerif Mardin and Binnaz Toprak. They try to explain the rise of Islamic movements on more scientific and realistic grounds, Erdoğan himself decisively rejects several assumptions of "paradigmatic error". He points out that "Islam.... is a formative component of Turkey's social and cultural fabric", not an outsider. Therefore, it will have appearence in Turkish politics and public debate in various forms unless it is not supperesed legally or politically." If it did not do so before 1950s, it was because appearances of religious faith and practices had been suppressed brutally. When Turkey chose to be democracy in 1950, the policy with respect to religion was bound to change. Democratization has inevitably led to the raising political participation of religious masses. This has become more evident during 1980s under the leadership of Turkey's late president Turgut Özal.

Though the secular elites of Turkey claim that modernization and secularism started with M. Kemal, the history of modernization in Turkey goes back to early 19th century. Erdoğan gives us a short story of Turkish modernization. His aim is to put the picture as a whole before the reader to show the continuity between the Ottoman Empire and Turkish Republic. He is brave enough to underline that the Turkish Republic has been even more backward in some respects than its predecessor. In the single-party period the ruling elite monopolized the political power and invaded all civil society domains including religious ones step by step.

In the first democratically held election of May 1950, the Democrat Party came to power with a huge majority in the Assembly. Democrat Party government was counter-attacked by the Kemalist elite who was controlling legal and institutional mechanisms. Republican People's Party made investment in the army to curb and if possible to throw away Democratic Party government from the power. Thus Turkey had its first military coup in 1960 which consolidated the grip of Kemalist elites upon the regime. The military interventions of 1971 and 1980 would follow the same path.

Meanwhile Islam had been gaining visibilitiy in social, cultural, political, and economic spheres. As a political movement representing Islamic demands it first appeared in 1969 under the flag of National Order Party. After this party's being closed down by the Constitutional Court, National Salvation Party came into existence. It was too closed by the constituonal court. (Interestingly its successor WP would also be closed at the same charges). Late president Turgut Özal's opening up the system widened liberties in political arena from which religios groups and religious masses benefited generously like all other segments of society. However all these were resenting the secular establishment.

After the death of Özal in April 1993, "the political atmosphere started to change and the military, through NSC (National Security Council), gradually reassumed the initiative in government policies", according to Mustafa Erdoğan. The military's dominance reached to its peak when it, again through NSC, forced the coalition government, between Welfare Party and True Path Party, out of office. It is out of question that the dominant power in Turkey in the end 20th century has been the military.

After this historical and actual account of Turkish politics Erdoğan turns to secularization adventure of Turkey. The subtitle he chose here speaks for itself: "Radical Secularization in Turkey". This title makes clear that Erdoğan sees the Turkish State's attempt to secularize the country-society as a radical step. To explain this he applies to the analitical tools developed by D. E. Smith and David Apter.

In his view, "Kemalist secularism restes not on the separation between religion and state but on government control over religion". He refers here to Levent Köker who pointed out that he Turkish state sought to replace Islamic value system with a "scientific one. Thus the Turkish type of secularism appeared as a radical one, to the extent that, the State tried to create a kind of political religion in the sense Apter put forward. The unique chacarter of creating political religion is this: It politicizes all life. In result politics as we know it disappears. Conflict that lies beneath politics becomes not only bod, but also counter revolutionary. This understanding, in Apter's words, "runs counter to the natural evolution of human society, and ideas of opposition downgrade and confuse the power of positive thinking. Ideas not only are dangerous, challenging the legitimacy of the regime or charisma of the leader. They also represent unscientific vestige wherever they run counter to those of the regime."

Thus M. Erdoğan finds most elements of political religion in Kemalist secularism. Among which are the monolithic character of state structure, monopolization of political power, single party to control society, charismatic leadership personifying the monistic character of the regime, and context of "Kemalist ideology". The author underlines one important point, that is, political religion can not be an end in itself. "The final objective of creating a political religion is to incorporate a new value system and code of conduct- a religion to replace traditional religion." In his view Turkey seems to have attempted "to replace Islam with a new civil religion that was to grow up from secular ideas and institutions." How successful it has been is of course open to debate. The rise of Islamic movements may suffice to say that this attemp has not been as successful as its initiators must have hoped.

Mustafa Erdoğan concludes with this: Islam is not only a religious faith, it is also a part of Turkish social, cultural, public, and political life. It is deep rooted in the Turkish society. There can be no oddness in the growth of Islamic revival during democratization process. This is not a pathological phenomenan. "Turkey's political elite has to learn to live with Islam. If Turkey really wants to be a democracy, it will do successfully only with Islam, not by attempting to cast it off".

Ahmet Aslan has the last article in this volume in which he discusses the compatibility between Islam and democracy. As a professor of classical Islamic philosophy by profession, he begins by pointing out the two sides of the longlasting debate. On one side there are those writers who confidently say "constitutional administration, secularism and human rights are not incongruous with the basic values and notions of Islamic civilisation." On the other side we see those who claim that these values "have no place in the religion of Islam, in Islamic culture and Islamic traditions." He counts among defenders of the second view Sayyid Qutb of Egypt, Abu'l Ala Mawdudi of Pakistan, Ali Shariati of Iran and Ali Bulac of Turkey.

He is now ready to eleborate both stances. The holders of first view mentions these as proofs or source of their convinctions: Coming of rulers to power through elections during the first four caliphs; ijma that "represents a compromise first among the scholars who have the authority to interpret the religion accurately and then among all muslims"; ulema's having "the authority to formulate the rules relating to the problems which may arise in the social life of all muslims." The absence of an istitution between God and man; Islam's egalitarian attitude with respect to race, language and social and economic position can also be counted among the elements supporting democratic principles. Aslan also summarizes the argument of those who see an incompatibility between Islamic traditions – values and democracy: Islam's not distinguishing between religious community and political community; its imposition of the Sharia'a as law and constitution that empowers religious scholars; the scholars' authority to refuse or challenge governmental policies. More handicaps are on the line like Islam's not recognising equality between genders or Muslims and non-muslims and the problems in political participation.

Aslan himself is a critic of both views. The first is too optimistic and the second to pessimistic. Looking at the actual politics in Islamic countries he observes: "... opposition movements carry the banners of democracy, human, and democratic values while they oppose existing despotic, autocratic regimes. On the other hand, enough sings exist to show that these movements or their spokesmen are not committed to democracy as a positive doctrine and a positive program."

He then turns to the case best known to himself: Turkey. He criticizes Necmettin Erbakan, the leader of former WP for taking democracy as a means to an Islamic end and for his majoritarian understanding of democracy. WP's lack of interest in the freedoms of other groups, individuals and minorities is rightly subject to his criticisms. Indeed the WP did not show a real concern with respect to basic universal human rights until itself came under pressure from the establishment.

In line with M. Erdoğan's argument, he points out that Turkish modernization and secularization process has a history of 150 years. This process culminated in democracy in 1946. In the last ten-fifteen years Turkey has made big progress in economy. In particular the development of civil society accelerated in 1980's with the liberalising policies of the late prime-minister (then president) Turgut Özal.

Naturally this has provided a ground for "the Islamic movements that have been wishing to express themselves more freely and in a more institutionalised form since the transition to democracy." The WP took advantage of this event to raise to the position of biggest political party in the country. In other areas also we witnessed the institutionalization of Islamic movements, like businessmen circles and women movements.

As Aslan rightly points out, woman-issue has occupied and will occupy Turkey's public agenda for some time: Women's wearing head scarf. This act has two sides: "On the one hand, this movement presents itself in radical opposition to modernity. On the other hand it also carries attributes of being a criticism, or oven a refusal of traditional Islam." It is interesting that "the demands for the right to wear Islamic dress are voiced with reference to, or associated with reference to, or associated with contemporary values such as individual freedoms, rather than Islamic references." The same it true also for Islamic writers and intellectuals in defending universal values. "In this context during the last ten years, the western school of thought that has been most popular with this group (of intellectuals) was post-modernism and the famous writers and representatives associated with it."

Aslan deals with prospects for an Islamic democracy in the last pages of his article. Despite not denying setbacks Islamic movements suffer from, he warns not to dismiss them totally as reactionary. He sees hopeful signs in Turkey that may be of help to the democratization of Islam or the emergence of, what he calls, "an Islamic version of democratic rule." However he again warns us that "we can not ignore those developments that run counter to this trend and indeed threaten it." Aslan believes that "life will teach all the parties the lessons of modern life and social order." Within this framework Islam and Islamist movements will be more compromising with democracy and democratic values as it has happened with Christianity.

You must have heard the saying: "All good things happen by accident and all bad things are well-planed." I think this is the case with this book. Despite the fact that the authors had been given just general subjects to write about, they came up with articles that perfectly combine with, and complete, each other. It would be nice if we found more reference to, or more interpretation of, Islamic sources and teachings in the articles of Barry and Kukathas as they both have been leading figures in political philosophy in the last decade. However, I suppose they have just made a beginning and we have many reasons to expect more from them in the future on the subjects they shortly dealt with here. The same goes, of course, for Detmar Doering. As a bright student of classical liberalism, he could contribute much more to the democratization of Islamic countries and to our better understanding of civil society-religion relations through his future work. Erdoğan and Aslan are leading intellectuals in Turkey and one can always find something new to learn in their work, as it is here.

I am particularly pleased that Barry and Kukathas have not been short of emphasizing the relation between civil society and market economy-society. This relation has been constantly ignored in civil society discussions because of the left wing authors have dominated for long time. The truth is clear: There can be no civil society in the absence of market economy. Thus one of the ways to promote civil society in Islamic countries is to promote market economy.

All authors agree on the importance religions carry in societal structure not only for the believers but also for whole society. This may be seen as a timely and important warning to those Islamic countries who carry secularism to radical extermist points. Liberal secularism does not aim at secularizing whole society, it just seeks secularization of politics. This is such an important point for Turkey nowadays that we need to remember it every day, if not everymoment. I would like to conclude with this. I am much more optimistic, after reading such a good collection of articles, about the future of democracy, civil society, and market economy in Islamic countries in general and in Turkey in particular.

CIVIL SOCIETY, RELIGION, AND ISLAM

Norman Barry[*]

The concept of civil society is closely associated with the post-communist era.[1] Although its intellectual roots are in the history of European liberal thought it was developed in Eastern Europe where countries struggling to be free of communism, yet reluctant to embrace wholeheartedly the perhaps excessive individualism of America, and to some extent that of Britain, sought a form of social order that encouraged civility and embodied a concept of freedom that was distinct from the pure economic liberalism that is such a feature of Anglo-American capitalism. To the proponents of civil society that is too redolent of the abstract individualism of market society, in which persons are identified merely by their preferences and not by any association with ongoing social orders. In pure market theory, persons are not inhabitants of any known social order and they lack any feelings of moral obligation to given, or received, institutions. For theorists of civil society, however, the market is morally validated only when it is embedded in institutions which have ethical justification independent of pure choice. In this context religion is very important for civil society since it provides just that framework of morality which binds individuals to one another by methods other than market exchange (even though civil society is formally secular). This is not to say that the great

---

[*] *Professor of Politics, Buckhingam University, England.*

1

religions of the world are all antithetical to the market or its essential component, the system of private property. With the perennial doubt about usury, which is shared by a number of the world's great religions, most of the features of the market were celebrated, for example in Islam and Roman Catholicism, long before they were elaborated by Adam Smith and the writers of the eighteenth century Scottish Enlightenment.[2] It is significant that the totalitarian features of communism were most significantly illustrated in its war against religion: a campaign conducted either by way of outright suppression or, more subtly, through the infiltration and subversion of religious institutions, as in the case of the Russian Orthodox Church. It is also true that the rudiments of civil society were developed in a religious context. Indeed, as the example of the Polish Roman Catholic Church shows, traditional religious institutions were the most resistant to communism. Civil society may have had its intellectual origins in the humanistic, if not atheistic, European Enlightenment era but even organised religion is by no means antithetical to its main features.

As for the specifically social and political elements of civil society, certain institutional prescriptions stand out. The most important of these is the rejection of centralised political arrangements which embody the features of Hobbesian sovereignty. The existence of a legislative body authorised to make all law in the form of commands backed by sanctions is alien to civil society.[3] The latter envisages a set of social arrangements, including legislatures, all of which are constrained by a higher law. Decisively, the legislature should be limited by law not of its own making.[4] This could be achieved either by a written constitution whose features cannot be changed by the conventional law-making process or by the idea of common law which may have equal validity with statute or has some protection from the potential ravages of the legislature. It is ironic that Great Britain managed to retain the main elements of civil society while having a sovereign parliament which contained the legal potentiality for the construction of a Hobbesian, all-powerful state.

What we have in the legal structure of civil society is the idea of the rule of law.[5] This is not simply technical legality, by which law is valid if it satisfies the criteria specified in formal procedures, but a more substantive constraint on law-making power: a constraint which elevates an independent judiciary to a crucially important position in the constitutional structure of the state. Communism had, of course, no respect for law in this sense. To its believers, traditional law was simply an arbitrary edifice for the protection of property. Under communism, individuals could expect no protection from law, it was simply part of the coercive administrative state.

In keeping with its anti-centralist doctrine, civil society envisages decentralised law and politics. The imposition of uniform plans across divergent communities was an example of the crass rationalism of the communist state. Just as in planned economies, there is no freedom to innovate and to make the best use of dispersed knowledge in statist legal systems. Only in conditions of liberty and the rule of law is there the possibility of the preservation and development of differing cultural arrangements, religious practices and moral traditions. They are, in effect, in peaceful competition with each other.

In civil society the ideal political form would be federalism (or even confederalism) in which particular communities could give vent to their differences (in language or

3

religion) within an overall structure of protective law. What is so important here is the right of 'exit' from a local community which does not meet with one's own cultural predilections. Of course, exit costs in politics might be quite high but the existence of the right to leave a community deters rationalistic rulers from imposing uniformity either in economic policy, welfare arrangements or in tax law. As in economics generally so in politics, a necessary protection for liberty is the possibility of variety and heterogeneity under impartial law.

In the modern world it cannot be said that the preservation of this feature of civil society has been successful. In almost all federal states there has been a tendency for the central government to acquire power and to impose uniformity. In America especially, the original protection of the autonomy of the states (guaranteed by the Tenth Amendment) has been whittled away by a succession of centralist measures (often to do with taxation, welfare and industrial and social regulation) which have subverted the intentions of the Founding Fathers.[6] Even in political systems which have preserved some decentralised powers there has been the practice of devolved legislatures behaving in a potentially oppressive way towards their minorities. In Quebec, the mainly French-speaking province of Canada, the majority there is not over-anxious to protect the language and other rights of the English speakers (and other minorities). There is always a tension in civil society between the claims for autonomy of devolved institutions in the promotion of variety and differentiation and the overall protection of basic rights for all citizens. Still, in the Canadian example, it is most unlikely the French-speaking Quebeckers will have their way of life threatened with extinction by the spread of English (and the Anglo-American culture) without

4

the protection of coercive Francophile laws; which is what they have introduced.

Civil Society and Liberalism

It should be clear that there is a close connection between civil society and liberalism: both doctrines proclaim individual freedom, minority rights and the protection of a legal system untainted by politics. They also have an antipathy to overarching social doctrines which claim that one way of life has an exclusive claim to political and constitutional supremacy over others. Both have a faith in the spontaneous working of individual choice in the determination of the good. No one conception should have priority over others. What has confused the modern debate is the perversion of the word 'liberalism', in America especially. Here it has lost its original foundation in free market economics in favour of an expanded conception of equality; a development that has licensed the state to engage in acts of intervention in the market which would have been anathema to nineteenth century economic liberals. The two versions, however, are united in their more or less subjective approach to moral values (except to justice which is agreed to have some objective foundation in reason, though its meaning is a matter of incessant dispute) and in their commitment to the priority of the right over the good.[7]

Liberalism and Religion

There is one area in which we are witnessing, in the late twentieth century, a further divergence between these two images of society. It is in religion, where the original *sotto voce* secularism of liberalism has taken on a more aggressive form. Of course, this is a long way from the enforced atheism of

5

communism but in certain circumstances it appears somewhat alien to the major tenets of civil society. In the constitutional debates, and Supreme Court decisions concerning the separation of church and state, in American society we can see, in embryonic form, a movement against the toleration of divergent social forces which is such a feature of civil society. Although America is a very religious country (at least in terms of church attendance and overt expression of faith) there is little or no opportunity for any of this to be expressed in its public institutions (especially its public schools). While it is true that both civil society and liberalism demand a separation between church and state the latter seems to make the wall completely insurmountable. It is one thing to forbid an established church, financed by taxpayers money and possessed of certain privileges, it is quite another to outlaw any minor expression of religious belief in the public sphere. Yet any reference to Christmas, Easter (or any other religious festival) and any minor acknowledgment of the Almighty through prayer are all prohibited because of the Supreme Court's somewhat convoluted interpretation of the Constitution. And this is true even if an overwhelming majority of parents are of one faith and desire some minor expression of this; and if children of a minority faith are not compelled to join in the religious ceremonies. It is often forgotten that the Constitution technically only forbids the federal government establishing a religion. It does not prevent the states having a public church, as a number did until the middle of the nineteenth century. Least of all does it prevent prayers in the public schools. Yet this is what has happened and it has been confirmed in a number of landmark cases before the Court.

Of course, there would be no problem if all the schools were private in America since they could then practice any religion without endangering the separation between church and state. Yet the extreme anti-religious campaigners do not press for the privatisation of schools. This might be because they do not wish to undermine the privileges of unionised schoolteachers in a socialized educational system, or because the liberal elite wants subtly to impose a form of secularism by stealth against the desires of the bulk of the population. Either way, it is not at all clear that this hostility to religion is consistent with civil society. Turkey is perhaps a better example here of a civil society since it does allow the teaching of Islam in the schools but this does not compromise the basic integrity of the secular state. For the state not to recognize the fact that the overwhelming majority of the population is of a certain religious persuasion, or to forbid public expression of it, is surely a breach of the principles of civil society.

There are other examples in America of what might be called 'liberal totalitarianism'. The usurpation by the Supreme Court of the states' rights to legislate on abortion is a breach of the commitment to legislative pluralism, which is a component of civil society. Of course, the debate between proponents of the woman's right to choose and those who stress the right to life can never be satisfactorily resolved. But the assumption of de facto legislative power by the Supreme Court in the *Roe v. Wade* case, which established the constitutional right to abortion, was an affront to those sections of American society which had serious moral and religious objections to the practice. The previous arrangement, by which the states themselves legislated on the issue, was no doubt intellectually unsatisfactory but it was more consistent with the ideals of civil society.

Rights

Indeed, the obsession with rights which ideological liberalism encourages marks a further difference from civil society, for in liberalism these rights are invariably thought to hold independently of the obligatory nature of social duty (apart from the minimal duty to respect the equal rights of others). Rights of this individualistic sort are commonly held to be divisive, they put up a barrier between the person and the community. Each of us is a rights-bearer with no reciprocal duties to care for the well-being of others. This divisiveness is compounded in American liberal society by excessive legalism: individuals are too anxious to settle their differences through the medium of the law and this litigious attitude has a corrosive effect on trust. In civil society, citizens can rely on each others' promises without the need to resort to law. In economic terms there are clear advantages to trust, its existence reduces transactions costs; most notably expenditure on lawyers.

Perhaps the most deleterious effect of the rights mentality has been in the welfare area. For the attribution of welfare payments to persons as of right, with no concomitant social duties, has been said to contribute to the rise of a socially-dysfunctional underclass in American inner cities, the collapse of the family and a general deterioration of the social fabric. A non-ideological civil society would foster those feelings of duty which are not encouraged by liberal individualism.

Liberalism, Civil Society, and Democracy

Yet despite these differences between civil society and liberalism, both doctrines share common intellectual roots and display similar concerns. It is especially true of their attitudes towards democracy. For despite the emotive appeal of this ideal in the postcommunist world it is certainly important to question some of its claims, especially in its majoritarian form. It has long been known in political theory that there is a difference between liberal democratic procedures and liberal democratic outcomes . The majority rule procedure is quite capable of generating illiberal states of affairs, especially in societies characterised by wide religious or other cultural differences. Most liberal democrats are as much concerned with the containment of power by constitutional means as they are with the question of who wields power. In particular, certain sorts of religious enthusiasms are as threatening to a rights-based liberalism as they are to a more communally-oriented civil society. In Britain we have the example of Northern Ireland to confirm this rather depressing analysis. While civil society will want to preserve religious commitments and affiliations it will want to prevent the domination of any one of these forms: religious liberty is as important as the religious experience. While religion turned out to be a crucially important defence against communism, civil society is always wary of the danger that religion itself might generate a new example of totalitarianism.

There is also a pernicious form of 'mass society' which has occasionally developed out of democratic institutions in the twentieth century. In this potentially destabilising social order there is little to bind individuals together, no decentralised social arrangements which can form a barrier against state power or alternative sources of loyalty and affection for individuals. In this scenario, alienated individuals become highly vulnerable to authoritarianism and totalitarianism. Communitarian critics of economic liberalism say that the market produces 'atomised' individualism[8] which encourages these phenomena (although there is no evidence at all that they are consequences of the free exchange system).

Theorists of civil society have similar misgivings about some aspects of unrestrained capitalism. That is why those countries that emerged from communist Eastern Europe were anxious to dissociate themselves from the Wall St. and City of London versions of capitalism, with their obsessive concern for shareholder value and entrepreneurial profit; and their indifference to the social consequences of the remorseless allocative processes of the market. Thus the model of the 'social market economy', in which raw capitalism is modified by statutory welfare for those unable to survive in the free exchange system; and the takeover method of industrial reorganisation is tempered by a concern for the effect that rapid economic change might have on the integrity of local communities. This hostility to 'corporate raiders' was as much reinforced by voluntary action against them as it was by formal legal restraint of their activities. Furthermore there was claimed to be a much more harmonious relationship between employers and trade unions than existed in the more adversarial attitudes that were said to pervade industrial relationships in American and British capitalism.

The reverence for private property, then, has as much a moral foundation in civil society as it does an efficiency rationale (although the allocative effectiveness of the market was never denied). The existence of private property provided a further barrier against the state and made it possible for individuals to exercise their freedom and autonomy, even though doubts were expressed about the ruthless individualism that capitalism might entail. Also, some non-socialist critics of extreme laissez-faire thought that the doctrine could degenerate into an all-encompassing ideology which was simply the reverse side of communism. Still, all had to agree that the private property/market system certainly prevented the state from exercising total control of people's lives, as had been the case under communism.

Islam, Liberalism, and Civil Society

At first glance, the social, economic, ethical, and political implications of Islam might seem unpromising for believers in either liberalism or civil society.[10] Superficially it seems to have features of authoritarianism or even totalitarianism: Islam is an all-embracing creed that provides its followers with certain and indubitable knowledge of ethics, law and religion. It seems to be at some distance form that pluralism which is such a feature civil society. Also important is the fusion of church and state in Islam and the injunction for the state to fulfil a certain purpose, i.e. the realisation on earth of the will of Allah. Certainly, that scepticism about fundamental ethical and political truth, which is a characteristic of some versions of liberalism, is absent in Islamic doctrine. On the contrary, it is characterised by an absolutism about fundamental values. The no doubt misleading public and political image of Islam, which is often of a fierce, uncompromising and highly illiberal doctrine with little tolerance for opposing views, has not been helpful; though it might be more accurate to describe the regimes so characterised as Muslim rather than Islamic. The difference here turns upon the fact that Muslim states are led by Muslims who might show only a nominal respect for their religion while Islamic states structure their legal and political orders around an application of religious and social doctrine, as expounded by the Prophet. An examination of this philosophy shows that it has many of the moral and economic properties of the free societies of the West. In economic matters, at least, Islam may be rightly be said to have anticipated theories that were to become standard in the liberal West. Indeed, it is the Muslim states that have done so much to discredit Islam, not the least because they have corrupted its true message by infecting it with some of the now most discredited social doctrines of Western intellectuals (including, of course, socialism).

A difficulty in understanding the political theory of Islam is that there is no one authoritative text that deals exclusively with forms of government or even with political obligation in general. It is the case that the Prophet did not prescribe any specific form of government and no specific political prescription is laid down in the Qur'an. Furthermore, the fragmentation of Islamic society in the modern world means that the basic principles of Islam have had to adjust to a variety of local circumstances. Adaptation to change according to political circumstances is by no means excluded by Islam but this political uncertainty does lead to complex and possibly unanswerable questions about appropriate constitutional forms. It may be the case that the Islamic order in seventh century Medina (established by the Prophet) was the first example of the modern state but a description of it leaves many political questions unresolved. One good example of this is the vexed question of whether or not Islam is consistent with modern ideas of liberal democracy.

However, this uncertainty about precise political forms directs us to the most important feature of Islamic political thought - the superiority of law over the state. And in Islam, the fundamentals of law or Shari'ah is decisively not a matter of opinion or subject to any variation. In this respect Islam can be shown to be quite consistent with some leading ideas of civil society and liberalism, especially when these doctrines are grounded in the certain knowledge of natural law (though it has to be conceded that the influence of objective natural law over modern Western political thought has diminished, perhaps regrettably, in the twentieth century). For there is a clear distinction in Islam between mere executive government, for which there is no precise recommendation, and law, which is unchanging and, in principle, perfectly universal.

Islam and Law

What is distinctive about Islamic law is that it is binding on everyone, including the rulers (whomsoever they may be). There is no conception of sovereignty, apart from the ultimate and final authority of God. The idea that law can be made and unmade at the will of the ruler, a notion that emanates from Hobbes and which has had an unfortunate influence on some aspects cf Western thought, is alien to Islam. Just as there is no theoretical role for a sovereign, there are, strictly speaking, no 'nation states'. Islam is a universal community, not divisible into particular communities identifiable by race or language, or any other merely contingent feature of human beings. Indeed, there is a nascent theory of political obligation in Islam which authorises disobedience to an executive ruler who breaches the injunctions of the Shari'ah.[11] In this doctrine we see some similarity between Islam and the ideal of the medieval Christian Commonwealth, another example of a potentially universal community in which everyone is theoretically bound by natural law. And Islam is just as decisive as Christianity is, if not more so, about the moral injunctions of natural law.

What is interesting, in the context of modern, classical liberal theories of law, is that law in Islam is discovered, not made.

This is, of course, a distinction made famous by Hayek and it is remarkable how Islamic conceptions of law bear a close resemblance to his jurisprudence. Of course, Hayek's jurisprudence is not quite of a natural law type, his liberal scepticism deters him from a commitment to absolute and universally binding principles, but his rejection of specific command as the sole source of law (indeed the sovereign's orders are a minor part of his jurisprudence) bears a close resemblance to Islamic legal thought. In the latter, the true meaning and interpretation of the Shari'ah is discovered by legal scholars just as for Hayek common law judges do not create law, they find it through an exploration of cases and customary practices (although the legal activism of judges in America has perverted this idea of discovery in the common law).

Understandably, Islamic law must be uncertain in some areas, although indubitable in its foundational prescriptions, and in this there is a role for adjustment to particular circumstances. But even here there is no role for sovereign legislatures. Nor is there a privileged role for a 'priesthood' in the precise determination of the law; and this was a definitive feature of medieval Christian conceptions of natural law. The necessary adaptations and interpretations are made by the Ummah (which includes non-believers), or 'community'.

Community, Democracy, and Islam

The Islamic idea of community is a little different from contemporary notions, for in the former it is, in principle, universal and not limited territorially or linguistically. It therefore has little of the relativism which is implicit in modern Western anti-individualistic conceptions of community. It is also true that in theory the Ummah has an important role in the choice of the executive ruler (Caliph) of an Islamic state.

We can now begin to see the connection between islam and modern democracy. The commitment to untrammelled majority rule is specifically precluded by Islam, just as it is in modern liberalism and civil society: for the determination of law cannot be left to the whim of possibly transient numerical procedures. As Lukman Thaib says: 'In Islamic affairs, numerical majority is not the orientation of truth, for the Qur'an has repudiated any such notion'. But yet there is a 'democratic' element in Islam as long as that is not understood in terms of mere numbers. There is an important role for Shura, or consultation in Islam; it was indeed a feature of the Prophet's rulership in Medina. There is an obligation of the executive ruler to take account of the opinions of the citizens and, although this is not reducible to the mechanical procedures of majoritarianism, it does ensure that government rests.upon a form of consent. In this respect it is in the same theoretical world as civil society, and is consistent with the constraints on the 'will of the people' that have always been a feature of liberalism.

Islam and Ethics

The foundational political concept in Islamic moral and social thought is natural law and the most important feature of this is equality. This is an ethical notion which has little or no connection with modern (non-classical liberal) theories of egalitarianism. All persons are equal in the sight of God and are not differentiated by race or creed. As the Prophet said: 'People are as equal as the teeth of a comb, there is no superiority of an Arab over a non-Arab except by virtue of piety'[12]. Muslims are bound by natural law to treat even their enemies as equals. Justice, in the procedural sense of treating each person in a fair manner, regardless of contingent factors, and not social or redistributive justice, is the defining characteristic of Islamic law. Certainly no religious difference justifies the relaxation of natural law. The problem of minorities within an Islamic state may seem intractable to outsiders, given the Islamic insistence that politics is not an autonomous activity but is inextricably bound up with the propagation of the faith. To quote Thaib again: 'The state must be moulded in Islamic patterns'[13]. However, this superficially illiberal statement must not be misunderstood, for those 'Islamic patterns' include an important element which is pluralistic. A good Muslim is bound to respect other religions and acknowledge the rights and liberties of their believers. A proper Islamic state limits to only a few areas the decisiveness of its law; for example, non-believers are prohibited from usury (itself a contentious issue in Islamic thought), they must acknowledge the executive authority of the Caliph and are compelled to make some contribution to defence costs. But non-believers are entitled to welfare.

Certainly, in history the proper Islamic state has exhibited welcome features of pluralism. From the beginning of political Islam in Medina, Jews were accorded equal rights and in the Ottoman Empire Jews, Christians, and Muslims lived under their own legal systems. Those believers in civil society, when faced with the problem of minorities, have not gone as far as suggesting that there should be rival legal systems and, as we have seen, an aggressive version of American liberalism seeks to impose its moral values on dissenting minorities. There is a nascent theory of competitive jurisdictions in extreme individualist thought and as we have noticed many writers have recommended the right of 'exit' from unwelcome legal orders but conventional liberalism, especially in America, presupposes the rightness of its doctrine. Yet there is genuine legal pluralism in Islamic thought.

Islam and Human Rights

It should be apparent from the above that it is not too difficult to read off a set of human rights in Islam which is not radically different from the Lockean tradition of the West. And indeed, in 1981 an important document was published, The Universal Declaration of Human Rights and Human Rights in Islam,[14] which put Islamic human rights theory in the context of contemporary rights talk. Western readers were no doubt surprised by the theoretical similarity between Western and Islamic approaches. Not only are justice and equality stressed as fundamental human rights but the conventional claims to freedom of thought and discussion (including religious freedom), to property, to dissent, non-discrimination (including any based on racial or sexual grounds) and free movement are listed. There is even a right to social security or welfare, itself a subject which has caused great controversy in the West and has divided liberals between 'minimal state' theorists, who reject the collective and compulsory provision of welfare, and egalitarian liberals who enjoin the state to provide a range of protective services, including poor relief, costly pensions, unemployment insurance and free medical treatment. It would seem that a similar debate about the nature of rights is going on in Islamic circles.

In one important respect Islamic rights differ from some versions of contemporary Western liberal rights. This is the stress on the correlation between rights and duties. In Islamic thought the possession of a right is dependent on the performance of a social duty.[15] There is an explicit rejection of the perhaps wild individualism which is a feature of some versions of Western liberalism. Just how such duties are to be defined, and how they are to be enforced, is not obvious but the connection between rights and duties is conceptual. Perhaps such conditions may vary from community to community, an approach which is consistent with the Islamic idea of adaptability and adjustment to particular circumstances. Certainly Western writers themselves are showing considerable dissatisfaction with the notion of 'dutiless' rights and the whole issue has become important with the social and family breakdown that has occurred as a consequence of the granting of welfare rights unencumbered by any social obligations, for example to work or to refrain from self-destructive behaviour.

Islam, Civil Society, and Western Liberalism

It is apparent that in theory there are similarities between traditional Western liberal values and Islam, even though the public image of Muslim states and the attitudes of certain political leaders belie this. If anything, Islam is closer to classical liberalism[16] than it is to the egalitarian American variant. Furthermore, the fusion of church and state is not necessarily inconsistent with the major tenets of civil society. Even though the Islamic state is obviously not secular in theory, there is no attempt to impose its belief system on others. In economic matters the commitment to private property and the market is decisive, entrepreneurship is encouraged and in theoretical Islamic law the tax obligations are really quite trivial in comparison to those in the West. In terms of economics, Islam can claim to have originated the theory of the free market not only a long time before Adam Smith but also ahead of the fifteenth century Catholic School of

Salamanca, whose members have come to be accepted as the first expositors of market allocation, monetary theory and subjective value. But the thirteenth Islamic writer historian and social theorist, Khaldun had discovered the theory of the market and nascent capitalism as long ago as the thirteenth century. There is a problem about the prohibition of usurious interest rates (the Riba) but not only was that a feature of other religions (including originally Christianity) but it is not clear that it forbids all payment of interest on monetary loans (a necessary feature of capitalist development). At most purely exploitative interest rates are forbidden but not those that contribute to the generation of productive capacity.

One might well ask: why has Islam not been recognised as part of mainstream liberal social and political theory since much of its doctrine is consistent with it? One answer might be that Muslim (as opposed to Islamic) states have pursued social and economic practices which are not derived from the Qur'an, and which are nationalistic, illiberal and sometimes socialistic. They seem to have acquired quite the wrong doctrines from the West and many ideas which are alien to the pure Islamic tradition.

Still, there is this emphasis on religion as a source of political duties which some theorists of civil society, with their emphasis on formal secularism, no doubt resist. Also, there is a genuine fear in the West of all-embracing doctrines. It is easy to show in theory that Islam does not license the imposition of religion in a totalitarian-like way but the explanation of this requires some subtlety and understanding. Again, Islam has not been attractive to the women's movement in the liberal West. The next stage of Islamic political thought should be devoted to explaining to Western liberals and theorists of civil society just what in Islam is consistent with the individualist tradition of the West and what is not. Western liberal writers would certainly benefit from knowing that certain crucially important features of Islam are perfectly consistent with their own doctrines.

Notes

1. See Adam Seligman, *The Idea of Civil Society,* New York, The Free Press, 1992.
2. For a description of the writers of the Scottish Enlightenment in the context of classical liberal theory, see Norman Barry, *On Classical Liberalism and Libertarianism*, London, Macmillan, 1986, ch.2.
3. The theory ultimately derives from Hobbes. For a critique, see H.L.A. Hart, *The Concept of Law*, London, Oxford University Press, 1961.
4. See F.A. Von Hayek, *Rules and Order*, London, Routledge and Kegan Paul, 1973.
5. See Norman Barry, *An Introduction to Modern Political Theory*, third edition, London, Macmillan, 1995, ch.2.
6. See J. Dye, *Federalism as Competition*, Connecticut, Lexington Books, 1989.
7. John Rawls, *A Theory of Justice*, (Cambridge, Mass, Harvard, 1971), made a famous case for the priority of the right over the good.
8. See Charles Taylor, 'Atomism', in *Philosophical Papers* II, Cambridge, Cambridge University Press, 1985.
9. For a general account of Islamic political theory, see Muhammad S. El-Awa, *On the Political System of the Islamic State*, Indianapolis, American Trust Publications, 1980.
10. For a general account of the Islamic theory of political disobedience, see Lukman Thaib, *The Islamic Polity and Leadership*, Malaysia, Delta Publishing Company, 1995.

11. Thaib, *The Islamic Polity*, p.79.
12. Quoted in Thaib, *The Islamic Polity*, p.90.
13. Thaib, *The Islamic Polity*, p.26.
14. See Majid Al Khan, 'The Universal Declaration of Human Rights and Human Rights in Islam', in Tahir Mahmood (ed) *Human Rights in Islamic Law*, New Delhi, Genuine Publications, pp.65-83.
15. G.G. Weerantry, 'Islam and Human Rights', in Mahmood, *Human Rights and Islamic Law*, p.17.
16. See Imad-ad-Dean Ahmad, 'Islam and Hayek', *Economic Affairs*, April, 1993, pp. 15-18.

ISLAM, DEMOCRACY, AND CIVIL SOCIETY

Chandran Kukathas[*]

What is the relationship between Islam, democracy, and civil society? This is the question which supplies the topic of this essay. Its purpose, more particularly, is to explore the place of Islam in the modern world-a world which contemporary writers increasingly try to understand by invoking the notions of democracy and civil society. But the occasion for this exploration has a more precise origin still. The issue of the place of Islam in the modern world is raised, more often than not, by writers and commentators for whom Islam is, above all, a danger. In geo-political terms, it is a danger to the West; in world-historical terms, it is a danger to modernity; and in philosophical terms it is a danger to democracy. For many, then, Islam stands is a relationship of tension with -if not complete antagonism to-democracy and modernity. It is a religion, and a philosophy, which is a throwback to the middle ages, and an obstacle to human progress.[1] It is, in the end, incompatible with any kind of liberal political order.

The concern of this essay is to argue that Islam is not the threat it is taken to be. But to understand why, it is necessary to acquire a surer grasp of the nature of democracy, of the relationship between democracy and civil society, and of the place of religion in the modern world. Only an understanding of these matters will allow us to appreciate the moral worth of Islam, and to see why it might be a source of strength rather than a danger.

---

[*] *Professor of Political Philosophy, School of Politics, University College, University of New South Wales, Australian Defence Force Academy, Australia.*

None of this is to suggest, however, that there are no problems associated with the working of Islam or, indeed, any religion in the modern would. A related task of this paper, therefore, is to reflect on these difficulties, and to try to understand to what extent they stem from the nature of faith, or of religion, or certain religious faiths; and to what extent they have their roots in the nature of modern society, and liberal democratic society in particular.

Civil Society

The exploration of these questions is best begun with an investigation into the nature of civil society. This term is now very much in vogue, though interpretations of its meaning vary cinsiderably. A part of the reason for this is that the adjective "civil" adds a content to the term which is anything but evident from the meaning of the word. What kind of a society is "civil" society, and what makes it different from society? One answer is, quite simply, nothing. Civil society is, straightforwardly, society; and there is much to commend in this answer, since it is, broadly, right.

Yet this in itself will not advance mattes very far since what remains unclear is what, precisely, is a society. So it is with this question that we must begin. A part of the answer is to say that a society is a form of association made up of people who belong to different communities or associations which are geographically contiguous. The boundaries of a society are not always easy to specify, since the contiguity of societies makes it hard to say why one society has been left and another entered. Nonethless, distinctions or boundaries can, to some extent, be drawn. Since all societies are governed by law, the move from one legal jurisdiction is, to some extent, a move from one society to another. This understanding has to be qualified, however, by the recognition that law is not always confined by geographical boundaries. For one thing, people moving from one region to another may still find themselves subject to laws whose long arms reach even into other countries. Tourists, businessmen, and `visiting scholars' remain subject to the laws of their home countries-especially to their tax laws. In the Middle Ages, the merchant law established codes of conduct and mechanisms of dispute resolution which bound traders who wandered across Europe-almost whereever they might be. And for another thing, an important dimension of law deals precisely with the fact that people cross boundaries into different legal jurisdictions all the time; much of law is interjurisdictional.

Yet this fact itself may help to get us a little closer to an account of what is a society. For a society surely exists when there is some established set of customs or conventions or legal arrangements specifying how the laws apply to persons whether they stay or move from one jurisdiction to another within the greater realm. On this understanding, there was not (as much of) a society among the different highland peoples of New Guinea in the nineteenth century since they lived in legal isolation from one another, even if they were aware of one another's existence. There was, however, a society in Medieval Spain, in which Jews, Muslims, and Christians co-existed under elaborate legal arrangement specifying the rights and obligations individuals had within their own religious communities, and as outsiders within the others.

It may be unwise to seek any greater precision than this in accounting for what is a society. For the moment at least, then, I will take a society to be a region of contiguous jurisdictions related by law. Societies can be distinguished from one another by jurisdictional separateness. This in itself may be a matter of degree, since some borders or boundaries are more porous than others. One particularly clear way in which societies may be distinguished is by their political separation. Thus we might talk of America and Mexico, or France and Germany as different societies. Yet the distinction cannot be drawn equally sharply, since France and Germany belong to the European Union whose laws permitting the free movement of people across borders have lessened the significance of the political borders in distinguishing the two societies. The United States and Mexico are, perhaps, more clearly distinguishable as separate societies-although the North America Free Trade Agreement may, eventually, have a profound impact on the nature of this separateness.

This account of the notion of a society is not an especially comprehensive one. "In particular, it says nothing about the cultural dimension of society. This, clearly, would add some important complications to the picture. For one thing, many political borders cut through regions in which peoples immediately on either side of the (new) boundaries have more in common with their neigbours than with their countrymen. The Kashmiris may feel more in common with each other than with their fellow Indians or with their fellow Pakistanis. And along the much-shifted borers of France and Germany live peoples who once saw themselves not as members of French or German society but as peoples of particular local regions. For the moment, however, I will ignore this complication to the description of society since it does not affect the argument to be presented here.

Yet something important is being said when the adjective "civil" is invoked to describe or qualify "society". According to Leszek Kolakowski, "civil" society is a whole mass of conflicting individual and group aspirations, empirical daily life with all its conflicts and struggles, the realm of private desires and private endeavours.[2] It is thus a complex association of individuals, joined together in relations shaped by personal interest, economic interdependence, and legal and customary rules. Within such an association would be found persons who associate with one another for friendship, or to pursue common goals, to exchange goods and idea. One would find churches, clubs, universities, businesses, and various bodies and practices which make up the institution of law. More importantly still, excluded from this realm are certain kinds of political relations: those which make up that entity called the state.

Civil society means society as distinguished from the state. This is not to say that the two are always separate, in fact, the distinction is a conceptual distinction more than it is an empirical one. But it is important nonetheless. And since the state is a relative modern phenomenon, whose emergence may be traced back no earlier then sixteenth century Europe, the term civil society identifies a distinctively modern form of society.

The notion of civil society also embodies another idea which is of singular importance: the idea of freedom. For civil society is a realm of freedom; but a freedom of a certain kind. Though this conception of freedom is not easily articulated, it is perhaps most readily grasped by appreciating what it is that Karl Marx, and Marxism in general, found so unsatisfactory about it.

Karl Marx was fundamentally a Rousseauean in social philosophy-one who reacted against the Philosophy of Right of Hegel to become a critic of civil society. Civil society ("bürgerliche Gessellshaft") in Marx's conception was bourgeois society-market society; and the relations which dominated it were relations of self interest and economic calculation. In this society, he argued, the one thing which could never be found was human freedom. Indeed, this form of society was nothing if not destructive of that freedom. In turning all human relations into mere money relations it would never allow men to attain the autonomy in which real freedom would consist. Civil society- capitalism- would sustain only heteronomy in a world of class conflict.

What one would find in such a society, Marx argued, was simply the satisfaction of particular, private interests-at the expense of other particular interests. But, unlike Hegel, Marx rejected as any sort of a solution an attempt at the reconciliation of interests. Hegel thought that the state would turn out to embody the general interest, reconciling the particular interests found in the family and civil society. For Marx, however, only the abolition of particularity was an acceptable solution. The state, he argued, would turn out to be nothing more than the agent of particular interests masquerading as the embodiment of the general interest. Politics in such circumstances is merely a conflict among particular concerns. The political rights or freedoms sought by those who would reform the state could not, in the end, bring freedom because "mere" political emancipation-the making of one's political attributes independent of the features of one's civil life (wealth, birth, religion) -was an illusory emancipation: "the state can free itself from a restriction without man being really free from this restriction"[3] Not only was political emancipation illusory, but it brought about a fundamental division in human life:

"Where the political state has attained its free development, man-not only in thought, in consciousness, but in reality, in life-leads a twofold life, a heavenly and an earthly life: life in the

political community, in which he considers himself a communal being, and life in civil society, in which he acts as a private individual, regards other men as a means, degrades himself into a means, and becomes the plaything of alien powers."[4]

Civil society was thus an expression of man's separation from his community and from his real self: an expression of his alienation. The only bond which holds men together in civil society, Marx argued, "is natural necessity, need and private interest, the preservation of their property and . their egoistic selves."[5]

Yet this view, at once, overestimates the possibility of human freedom, and underestimates (and underappreciates) the freedom found in civil society. Indeed it misunderstands civil society altogether. While Marx was right to see civil society as the realm of particularity, he was quite wrong to think this could ever be abolished, or to imagine that the conflictless utopia of postcivil society was anything but a grotesque illusion. Any plausible notion of freedom must offer an account of how conflict and difference can be accommodated -for they surely cannot be overcome.

The freedom embodied in civil society is the freedom that allows human beings to live together in spite of their differences and in spite of the conflicts which arise from their varying interests, temperament, and beliefs. And this understanding of freedom is what makes civil society a notably modern idea, for at its core is a recognition that in human society, nowadays, people worship different god, and that this fact has to be accommodated by legal and political institutions if humans are to stand any chance of flourishing.

This last point also reveals another important feature of civil society-one whose salience is unappreciated (if recognized at all) by Marx's analysis. Civil society is peopled not by isolated or separate individuals but by associations or communities. Civil society is market society; but it is not just market society. The associations within it include not only businesses but also, more importantly. associations to which people have attachments rooted less in their economic concerns than in their emotional attachments and moral commitments and so, in their identities. The most important associations or communities, here, are religious ones.

These associations are important because it is through them that people pursue the goals that give meaning to their lives. Indeed, it is through them that they seek understanding of what has value and of how they should seek it. It is through such associations that people seek understanding of their place in the world. For thinkers such as Marx and his followers, such attachments, particularly when they had a religious character, were an excrescence, revealing the absence of real human freedom in the world of particularities that was precommunist society. Human beings needed liberation from such attachments. The irony is that the philosophy which decried man's alienation and isolation in civil society failed completely to appreciate that it was precisely these particular attachments in civil society that people were made human; it was here that they were "civilised.

Democracy

Yet human beings are not only social creatures; they are also political ones, In Aristotle's world-the world of the city-states of ancient Greece-the social and the political order were one and the same. Community was political community; and diversity was not to be found, or welcomed, within the polis.[6] In the modern world, however, civil society is a realm of many associations, and one in which different gods are worshipped in different ways. The political problem under these circumstances is to work out how this is possible. It is no longer a problem of how to preserve unity; for such unity does not exist. It is a problem of how to make possible-and preserve-freedom: the freedom to live, and worship, differently.

What political institutions, then, are appropriate for such a condition? While it is tempting to reply, at once, democratic institutions, this answer is not self-evidently the right one. For one thing, not all circumstances may be conducive to democracy, since democracy is also a practice which has to be learned and may be a tradition which is unfamiliar or foreign to some peoples. But, more importantly, there are many kinds of models of democracy, and anyone advocating democracy must specify the type.

All this is to say that explaining what kinds of political institutions are suitable for a modern society-for civil society-will involve a more complex response. To begin this response it is necessary to turn again to the question of civil society, and to ask what it is about civil society that is the proper object of political concern. If civil society is a realm of many communities or associations, each pursuing its understanding of the good life (or, in the case of some, in search of such understanding), what matters most is the preservation of the freedom each needs to get on with the business of life. Yet the problem is that co-existence is no easy matter, since differences here will not simply be matters of taste but will raise questions about what is right, and how one should live. What is to be done?

Broadly speaking, two kinds of solutions have generally been proposed. One has been to say that the question of how one should live should be settled (at least to the extent of specifying what is not permissible) and the answer then imposed (gently, if possible) on all. Another has suggested that any solution to the problem of coexistence would seek no more than a modus vivendi, which did not attempt to solve the problem of how one should (or (should not) live, but looked to provide a framework of meta-norms[7] by which different ways could co-exist. The problem with the first solution is that it does not take seriously the fact that people disagree and will resist attempts to impose beliefs or practices upon them. This solution requires the use of power, the oppressive use of state power- to be precise.[8]

The second answer, however, is very conscious of the fact that disagreement is inevitable-and, possibly, ineradicable -and wary of the use of state power to enforce agreement. This is the answer which is appropriate for modern, civil society.[9] What is needed are political institutions which will tolerate the diversity of communities, associations, and traditions which are to be found in civil society. This anwer is a political philosophy most commonly labelled liberalism.

Yet so far all that has been said specifies only the moral principle which should underpin the political institutions which govern civil society. Nothing has been said about what kinds of institutions these should be. Liberals generally are concerned to ensure that the major institutions which deal with differences among people -law and government-do not unduly favour any particular way of life. However, even if this point is accepted in principle, the problem is that, once institutions are in place, those who operate them can often manipulate them to their advantage.

For this reason, it is wise to devise or put in place institutions which make it difficult for power to be concentrated. A good political order is therefore one in which power does not exist unopposed.

The ways in which power might be kept checked are many. In medieval Europe kings were bound in complex systems of reciprocal obligations to feudal lords, who in turn owed duties of their own to the people who lived on their lands. In the sultanates of pre-colonial Malaya, the activities of the Rajas were constrained by the understandings of the duties of ruler to subject woven through Malay political culture.[10] And in England, monarchical rule became more and more carefully circumscribed as Parliament arose, and grew to dominance, out of the late middle ages.

In the modern world, one very important political tradition whose point is to institutionalise the separation of powers is the tradition of democracy. Modern democracy has grown out of the political traditions which were transformed over the past three centuries by the emergence of industrial commercial society in Europe. Theoretical expression was given to this development most powerfully by the American thinkers of the eighteenth and nineteeenth centuries, though particular mention has to be made of the exceptional contribution of Tocqueville in his own analysis of American society. What most needs remarking on, here, is that the understanding of democracy which came to light in this time did not see democracy as majoritarianism, or as embodying the will of the people (though this thought did enter into some conceptions of democratic government). Democracy was conceived as a system of government in which there was, above all, freedom to oppose. Democratic governments were not free to do as they pleased but were open to challenge. A democracy was a regime, and a regime suited, most importantly, to an open society in which power was checked by other powers, and also by the capacity of nongovernmental institutions to examine and criticize the instruments of rule, and the rulers themselves. In a phrase, democracy, in its modern incarnation, presupposed freedom under law, it presupposed civil society.

Religion

The question it is now open for us to consider is, what is the place of religion in such a society? This is an important question in part because the traditions of liberalism and democracy described thus far are features of a modernity which has distinctly secular character. Liberal democracy, the child of European civil society, looks to be secular creed which can have no place for religion-unless it be a place of confinement and subordination.

Yet this is not the case. Indeed, it cannot be the case; even though the modern world is, in some important ways, thoroughly secularised. We need to understand how the world has indeed become more secular; but we need also to appreciate why, and how, religion has an important place in modern civil society.

The secular nature of modernity is most in evidence in the character of public discourse, not only in international society but within the public arenas of most societies. This reflects not only the dominance of science in discussions of the natural world, but also its domination in the world of human society. The languages of economics, sociology, and management have no need of any appeal to providence or divine intervention to account for the workings of human society, or to justify public action. Charles Larmore has suggested that this secularization is the consequence of the entrenchment of the monotheistic traditions of Judeo-

Christianity, which conceives of God as a single, transcendant entity. A transcendant God, he argues, has no place in explanations of the order of nature or the course of history. "Once we have resolved to let God be God, we can no longer use God for our own cognitive ends."[11] God is not dead; but we don't seem to need him- or want him-for most of what we do.

.   The secularization of the world in this sense is not only evident but also, in many ways, advantageous (though not strictly necessary, as I will explain presently). In a world in which different gods are worshipped, but in which adherents of different faiths interact in a global arena, anything but a secular public realm could be a disaster. Social intercourse with those who differ from us in profound ways requires that we prescind from our deepest commitments. Otherwise, the most likely outcome is conflict.

Yet none of this means that religion has no place in modern society-or that that can only be a matter of private individual commitment. For one thing, it ought to be noted that, even within the secularizing tendency of modernity, and the disenchantment of the world which has seen the emergence of Weber's legal rational mode of domination, the sacred has a powerful grip on human sensibilities. In part this is reflected in the persistence of faith, and the advance of religious organizations. But it is more powerfully evident in the human capacity to turn persons and objects into sacred entities: to hallow what was once devoid of meaning. So millions mourned not only the death of an Iranian cleric, and the passing of a Catholic nun, but also the demise of a faithless princess.

Religion will have a powerful place for as long as this sensibility is there, for there will be a demand for means of giving it expression. And while some will decry this fact as evidence of the persistence of the irrational in human activity, that will make no difference.

This last observation, however, brings us to a more important point. Reason alone is not going to be the guide for human beings in all things-however much some might think that it ought to be.[12] Indeed, it cannot be; for unaided reason cannot teach us anything substantive about value or morality about how to live. This, in spite of the best efforts of some of the great philosophers of the Enlightenment, and their modern successors, to generate a rationalist ethics. But this leaves us with the problem of how to pursue moral questions-how to think morally-if reason is not enough. This is a problem which confronts modernity, and which has to be faced. Any plausible response has to reject two preferred solutions. The first is in the suggestion that we look to nature to discover what it is that can properly be the object of value, and can form the foundation of a universally acceptable understanding of good conduct. The problem with this solution is that it is the fact that naturalism generates disagreement rather than consensus. The second is the empty promise offered by postmodernism, which, as Larmore points out, "ends up confusing the rejection of philosophical rationalism with the abandonment of reason itself."[13]

If reason alone is not enough, and the extremes of naturalism and postmodernism offer no solution, upon what resources can we draw to address our fundamental concerns in matters of value? One answer worth considering is that we turn to tradition.[14] This is, in fact, what we do depend upon. We do not try to generate moral judgements or solutions out of nothing, but begin with starting points given by our own contexts-by our traditions. These traditions embody our (various and diverse) understandings of what has aesthetic and moral worth; of what is worth aspiring to and what is taboo; of what is sacred and what is profane. And it is here that the place of religion is to be found.

All of us live within, and are guided by, particular traditions. These vary from culture to culture, from community to community, though there is often some overlap, our traditions tell us what is right, and what has value; and even when we disagree with their injunctions we start from those injunctions themselves. What has also to be appreciated, however, is the extent to which religion has shaped and continues to shape the traditions which dominate modern society. Religion has, in fact, performed two important functions.

First, it has been a source of substantive judgements on matters of value. Religious teaching is, for many, the source of understanding of what is worthy, and what is right, The religious imagination has been of critical importance in our efforts to understand and appreciate what is good. As economists might put it, religion generates moral capital.

Second, religion, in this way, has played an important role in constructing the understandings which have socialised individuals. Once again, we can see this if we reflect on Marx's misunderstandings in his analysis of "The Jewish Question". For him, religion was alienating, for it kept human beings from becoming truly human; but the conception of the human in Marx's thought is only an abstraction devoid of substantive content. And content is particular, not universal. Religions everywhere are human creations which have responded to the circumstances and needs of particular peoples. Even when they have attempted to universalise human ewperience they have responded to the particular experiences of the communnities they served.

If these two points are correct, than religion has an important place in civil society. This is not because it shapes the character of civil society directly, but because within the communities which comprise it is the religious imagination to which people will turn to answer the most important questions that confront them.

This brings us immediately, however, to a more pressing political question: what is, and should be, the political place of religion in civil society, and democratic civil society in particular. More precisely, what place should be accorded, in all of this, to Islam.

Islam

There are two views about the place of religion in modern society which ought to be rejected. Both come out of the European Enlightenment. The first suggestes that religion ought to be repudiated as irrational. Even if religious persecution is not to be condoned, religion should be scorned and its demise hastened. The second suggests that religion should be recognized as something important to some people, and therefore tolerated within tightly defined limits. This is one kind of liberal view which asserts that religious faith and practice is acceptable provided it is not inconsistent with more fundamentally important commitements a good society should have to upholding individual autonomy. Religious communities should be required to conform to these values, and permitted to practice within the bounds that these values demarcate.[15]

The first view should be rejected partly because it fails to recognize the centrality of religious faith and experience to so much of human society. But it is also of doubtful value because it says nothing about what might be put in its place. The cognitive and the socialising roles played by religion are not considered.

The second view, however, is more difficult to deal with. It does not seek to eliminate religion but to liberalize it. What is wrong with this? To be sure, adherents of particular religious faiths may not wish it; but that in itself is not an argument, since those who wish to liberalise illiberal practices think it would be a good thing, whether or not it is welcomed. The problem, however, is that this inclination is inconsistent with a proper understanding of the nature of civil society.

Civil society, as it has been described here, is a realm of diversity and difference. It is marked less by unity than by contestation and disagreement-albeit a form of contestation which is peaceful. It is, in many ways, a notably modern idea; for it is a feature of a world in which people not only worship different Gods but also do so in remarkable propinquity. What matters for the preservation (and flourishing) of such a realm is that it not be brought under control. Not even under liberal control. Civil society has to remain a realm of mutul toleration in which no particular tradition assumes the authority to shape the others. And this means that religion-even religion which does not accept this principle-has to be free.

It is at this point, however, that objections arise, and in particular objections which invoke the spectre of Islam. If religion is not kept in check it will devour civil society. And Islam, more than any other, the argument goes, is the likely predator. What needs to be considered now, then, is why this concern should be repudiated, particularly with respect to Islam.

It should be conceded at the outset, however, that religion can be a powerful and dangerous force in society. One of the most important reasons why this is so is that religion, by its nature, seeks and attracts followers. Those who are capable of mobilizing people in large numbers have great power in their hands. For this reason, rulers have generally sought to ally themselves with, or control, the religious institutions of their societies. Equally, religious leaders have often been tempted to use the power conferred by their authority to extend their influence into politics-sometimes even to take political power.

But while religion can become a political force, two things ought to be noted before any response to this fact is considered. The first is that this is no worse than any other group possessing an ideology coming to power. The danger is posed by the concentration, or usurpation, of power, and by the inclination of it possessors to use it. The second is that it is important to consider what might be the alternative to allowing religion to emerge as a political force. If the alternative is to concentrate political authority in the hands of a power great enough to keep all, including religion, in awe, the cure might be worse than the potential disease.

Indeed, in some respects, a society with strong religious institutions is to be preferred if what this means is that the power of the state is thereby checked. While it is right to be wary of the power religious authority might exert tyrannically if allowed, it bears noting that the greatest tyrannies in this century were exerted by the godless states of communism, and by Germany under the influence of Nazi doctrines of religious hatred. And it is worth remembering that religion provided not only a source of sanctuary in many of these societies, but also the source of resistance (the Polish Catholic church in the 1980s, for example).

In general, it may be a good thing if there exists a tension within society between church (or mosque) and state, provided that neither can clearly take the upper hand, or manipulate the other to its own ends. The greater the dispersal of power the better. This is, fundamentally, what the theory of pluralist democracy advocates: institutional arrangements in which the existence of a diversity of powers or authorities operates to constrain any one power from assuming a position of such preeminence that tyranny becomes a possibility.

Yet does this also hold for Islam, or is it a religon whose doctrines or character are such that it cannot coexist with any other power, and which is therefore suppressed if it gathers any kind of strength which might translate into political activity? Some have argued that the nature of Islam's traditions make it unlikely to tolerate such a political order. After all, the argument goes, Islam does not recognize any separation between mosque and state, or the notion of a secular authority. Could such a religious tradition be anything but a threat to a democratic order? And could it possibly embrace democratic traditions if it were in a position of dominance?

In fact, Islam is not the problem it is often presented to be, even though it is true that there have been Muslim tyrants as many, perhaps, as there have been Christian, or Hindu, or secular ones. Islam is not at odds with democracy or with civil society, or modernity. The key to understanding this is appreciating that Islam recognizes that a religion cannot embrace the whole of society for as long as there are unbelievers. It has therefore, from the outset, concerned itself with the question of the treatment of those who dissent from its teachings.

The earliest Muslim community or ummah had its origins in the seventh century as a persecuted minority in Mecca. As is well-known, Muhammed and his followers eventually left Mecca for Yathrib, or what is today Medina, in order to establish a community of the faithful. However, when the success of Muhammed's mission saw the expansion of the Islamic community, it was itself forced to address the question of how to deal with the diverse people, and what forms of diversity to accept in its midst. Its response was to develop a political tradition which was remarkable for its tolerance of non- Muslim communities.

Islam today, particularly in the west, conjures up images of fanaticism and intolerance. Yet much of its history is at odds with this impression. In the eighth and ninth centuries the Byzantine empire crumbled under the force of Islamic expansion, and Muslim armies eventually overran the Persian empire before also taking the regions of Syria, Iraq, North Africa, southern Europe and Spain. These areas, many of which were already subjugated to foreign rulers (particularly in Byzantine and Persian territories), were resubjugated to Islamic ones. Yet Islamic vision, for the most part, proved more reasonable and tolerant, and more willing to grant its subject populations a measure of local autonomy with lower rates of taxation. To Jews and Christians it accorded greater toleration than they had been accorded hitherto. Indeed, the local Christian churches had even aided the invading Muslim armies to escape the persecution for "heresy" they had endured at the hands of the "foreign" Christian orthodoxy.[16] The Muslim rulers left existing governmental institutions intact, and left religious communities free to govern their own internal affairs according to

42

taking the regions of Syria, Iraq, North Africa, Southern Europe and Spain. These areas, many of which were already subjugated to foreign rulers (particularly in Byzantine and Persian territories), were resubjugated to Islamic ones. Yet Islamic vision, for the most part, proved more reasonable and tolerant, and more willing to grant its subject populations a measure of local autonomy with lower rates of taxation. To Jews and Christians it accorded greater toleration than they had been accorded hitherto. Indeed, the local Christian churches had even aided the invading Muslim armies to escape the persecution for "heresy" they had endured at the hands of the "foreign" Christian Orthodoxy.16 The Muslim rulers left existing governmental institutions intact, and left religious comminities free to govern their own internal afairs according to their own faiths. To be sure, these rulers sought to eliminate idolatory and paganism, and regarded Islam as the one ture religion. But the Islamic ideal demanded that others be invited-persuaded-to convert, not forced. If they refused, they were to be left in peace. This was most notably so in Jerusalem, which had been captured by Muslim armies in 638. Under Muslim rule not only were Christian churches left unharmed, but Jews, long banned from the city by Christian rulers, were allowed to return-ushering in several centuries of peaceful coexistence, brought to an end only by the Crusades.

The point of noting all this, however, is not to insist that Islam's history is stainless, or that chose of its rivals are bloody. Like any tradition with a history spanning centuries, it has had its periods of stagnation as well as its periods of flowering. And those traditions have varied from the harshly austere, to the poetic mysticism of Sufism. But the point here is simply to make clear that there is no inconsistency between Islam and traditions of tolerantion and peaceful coexistence. Within Islam's traditions, as various scholars have argued, we find not only the practice of toleration but also the concepts which give it theoretical expression: concepts of oposition and disagreement, consensus and consultation, and freedom of thought and expression.

Like that of any doctrine, Islam's humanity and capacity for toleration depends on questions of interpretation. In the Qu'ran the injunction to struggle to defend Islam (jihad) is capable of many interpretations-but not all consistent with the use of armed force to persecute non-believers. In the same way, the biblical injunction to "compel them (non-Christians) to come in" to the Christian fold (Luke, XIV, 23) was capable of being interpreted by St Augustine as sanctioning righteous persecution even though Pierre Bayle would maintain that "compel" could only mean "persuade".

Given its nature and traditions, then, there is nothing in Islam that should give us cause for concern if our interest is in the flourishing of a democratic civil society marked by diversity. This is not to say that Islamic political movements have not, or will never, pose any danger. For any political movement can be dangerous. But it is to say that Islam as a creed is not the problem, and may even hold within it some of the resources that supply a solution. Most important among these resources is the tradition of toleration; but not less significant may be the fact that, in the end, it is also distrustful of nationalism.

If all this is true, the real question which ought to be addressed is not so much the problem of reconciling Islam with modern democracy and civil society as the prolem of what model of democracy is most suited to modernity. If the considerations presented in this paper are sound, what should give us most concern is the emergence of models of democratic governance which seeks to extend the power of democratic authority into supranational institutions, ordered in hierarchical fashion.[17] If democratic institutions are to work to preserve the diverse order of civil society, they will have to look away from models of centralization towards those traditions which are ready to embrace norms of toleration. In this regard, however, the threat comes not from Islam, even though it may at times come from those to misuse its name.

Notes

1. For examples of articles wary of Islam, see the list offered by John L. Esposito, *The Islamic Threat: Myth or Reality?* (New York: Oxford University Press, 1993), p.viii. (Esposito's book, it should be made clear, is sympathetic to Islam.)

2. "The Myth of Human Self-Identity: Unity of Civil and Political Society in Socialist Thought", in C. Kukathas, D. Lovell, and W. Maey (eds.), *The Transition from Socialism: State and Civil Society in the USSR* (Melbourne: Longman Cheshire, 1991, pp.41-58, at pp. 42-3,

3. Karl Marx, "On the Jewish Question", in Karl Marx and Frederick Engels, *Collected Works* (London: Lawrence and Wishart, 1975), vol.iii, pp.146-74, at p.152.

4. *Ibid.*, p.154

5. *Ibid.*, p.164.

6. On this see Arlene W. Saxonhouse, *Fear of Diversin: The Birth of Political Science in Ancient Greek Thought* (Chicago: University of Chicago Press, 1992)

7. For an interesting argument couched explicitly in terms of "meta-norms" see Douglas J. Den Uyl and Douglas B. Rasmussen, *Liberty Defended: The Challenge of Post-Modernity* (Nortliampton, MA: Edward EIgar, 1997)

8. The phrase is used in John Rawls, *Political Liberalism* (New York: Columbia Univers Press, 1993).

45

9. Much more needs to be said in justification of this claim than can be offered here. For a cogent, though controversial, defence of a variant of this position see Charles Larmore, *The Morals of Modernity* (Cambridge: Cambridge University Press, 1996), pp.121-74.

10. On this see A. C. Milner, *Kerajaan: Malay Political Culture on the Eve of Colonial Rule* (Tucson: University of Arizona Press, 1982)

11. Larmore, *op.cit.*, p.41.

12. See, for example, George H. Smith *Atheism: The Case Againts God* (Los Angeles Prometheus Books, 1973).

13. *Op.cit.*, pp. 55-6. The thinker Larmore has in mind here is Jean-Fraçois Lyotard. From a healty distrust of simplifying myths, argues Larmore, Lyotard infers that moral thinking must be combative and rhetorical rather than reasoned. But this is a non sequitur which "fails to escape the terms of the rationalistic idea of reason it attacks".

14. Once again, it is a thought which comes from Larmore, *op.cit.*, pp. 55-9, though I am adapting it for my own purposes.

15. For a powerful exposition of this view see Deborah Fitzmaurice, "Autonomy as a good", *Journal of Political Philosophy* 1 (1), 1993, pp.115.

16. On this see Esposito, *The Islamic Threat*, p. 39.

17. See for example the arguments offered by, David Held. *Models of Democracy*, 2nd ed. (Cambridge: Polity, 1996).

RELIGIONS AND CIVIL SOCIETY

Detmar Doering[*]

In his oriental Novel "Zadig, ou la destinée. Histoire orientale" of 1748 Voltaire presents one of his characters, Setok, the Arabian merchant, as a staunch defender of the old custom of burning widows along with the remains of their deceased husbands: "Since more than one thousand years it has been a tradition to burn widows. Who could dare to change a law hallowed by such a long validity! Is there something more venerable than an old abuse?"

Of course, Voltaire meant to ridicule traditional religion with this innocent remark. The little story almost archetypically presents a major strand of Western thought. The basic position is this: Religion and Civil Society do not go well together. Enlightened opinion in Western Europe has held this belief ever since the days of Voltaire. Images of the Spanish Inquisition torturing alleged heretics, crusades that brought war and misery over what then was seen as the known world, and an orthodoxy that thwarted the progress of science - all this to many people was (and still is) the consequence of religion when it gets what it wants to get - hold of political power. Without the advent of secularism, it is feared, we would still have religious wars, still burn witches at the stake, and still believe that the earth is a flat disc.

There were, of course, many conservatives, who were highly critical of this view. Religious truth, they said, could be reconciled with a secular concept of politics. Moreover, without religious

---

[*] *Director of Liberal Institute, Berlin, Germany.*

foundation no political system and no society could be sustained. They declared with Edmund Burke, that "man is a religious animal" and without religion man would degenerate and act against his nature. Civil society and the state, therefore, should not be completely separated from their religious foundations. "God willed the state", Burke said in 1790. Without it there would be no social cohesion. Much of this argument has become *en vogue* in recent years. Communitarians like *Alasdair MacIntyre* ("After Virtue", 1985) today lament the loss of moral and religious unity that was characteristic of the medieval world - a world that has been deliberately destroyed be the secular individualists.

There is, of course, some truth in both arguments. Western civilisation and western civil society certainly owes much its progress to some kind of secularism. On the other hand we see that the loss of social cohesion sometimes undermines even the most elementary rules of civil society.

The problem behind this conflict can only be solved if we start to define more clearly what is meant by "civil society".

The classical liberal - and at the same time most clearly stated - formula came from *John Locke*. A civil society is formed when people "unite for the mutual preservation of their lives, liberties and estates, which I call by the general name - property", Locke writes in his "Second Treatise of Government" of 1690. In this quite radical meta-political position civil society is defined by a political framework that only legitimately exists if it guarantees what we today would call the concept of "self-ownership". This concept can certainly claim universality in the light of common reason. In fact, it is very difficult to argue that you are not serving some very particularist interest if you decide to use collective or individual coercion that goes beyond this principle. In this context it does not even matter that Locke gives a theological foundation to his theory, namely that God has given men the faculty of reason to recognize the basic premises of civil society. The whole theory can very well work without this assumption.

In fact, the attempt to reconcile this notion of civil society and religion the quasi-Lockean way has never proved to be very successful. It is, of course, logically consistent (if not tautological) if you set the axiomatic premise that the liberal vision of the rights of man and religion are identical, and then conclude that, therefore, no contradiction exists between them. The whole of the 18th century is full of such attempts to create a "natural theology" out of nothing. Although it has to be admitted that these attempts had some positive influence on the established religions in Europe eliminating some of their more intolerant features in practice, they could never establish themselves as religious alternatives with a standing of their own.

The problem of finding a religion that can provide the underpinnings of a pure theory of liberalism is that the liberal vision of a civil society is an open process, not an end state. A liberal "natural theologist" can claim that he loves religion "in abstract" (and then he still may be confronted with the challenges of atheism), but he can not advocate any concrete "real-world" religion as an ultimate end that justifies coercion. Of course, a religion that can be really practised is always a concrete "real-world" religion. Those who honestly believe in a certain religion, say Islam, would not believe that it is sufficient for the salvation of their souls to know that liberalism, to put it in the terms of typically liberal economic theory, has "offered to the individual an increase in the area of choice". Since religion is mostly concerned with end states, their choices have already been made. Hence their an "increase in the area of choice" to them is rather pointless, if not immoral. This explains why most religion at one stage of their historical development tended to advocate (and exercise) intolerant legislation to enforce their specific moral and religious standards, such as dress codes for women or the prohibtion to eat meat on Friday.

Nevertheless, it has to be recognised that the religion's concern for "end states" can have positive consequences, too. After all, being concerned with specific end states is a necessary condition of human life. You cannot even go shopping, you cannot eat, you cannot drink without making exclusive, non-universal choices. What is worse, you cannot even educate. It is clear that people by nature do not always stick to the rules of civil society. They may easily turn into selfish aggressors. Hence education is somehow necessary, otherwise the most perfect liberal order would instantly collapse. Here too, no education "in abstract" is possible. You always have to learn and internalise a concrete way of behaviour not a "behaviour as such" or tolerance for various types of behaviour without adopting one for yourself. Some writers, therefore, have argued with good arguments, that concrete "real-world" religions have a very useful role to play in delivering the stable substructure of a civil society. Sometimes, in deviation from the Lockean definition, this substructure of "living experience" is itself seen as *the* civil society.

Paul Johnson, the British historian, has remarked: "The fact is that the practice of religion is the most effective, and by far the cheapest and least oppressive, form of social control ever devised. Hence attempts by the state to eliminate it have inevitably contributed to social irresponsibility, reflected in high illegitimacy rates and crime."

Such an argument invites the conclusion that a liberal civil society offers no concrete moral values to teach. This is, of course, incorrect. There are many values which are even considered to be absolute in such a civil society, such as the inviolability of property or the abiding of contracts. However religion and other forms of "social control" are helpful to make a civil society work smoothly. There is, of course, an air of cynicism behind this argument. Although it is highly in favour of religion, it is in reality totaly secularist. It is, in fact, a utilitarian theory of religion that admits no immanent value to religion as such. As a consequence of this, Paul Johnson continues quite revealingly: "Secular humanism and other forms of non-religious morality may work for the highly educated, privileged, high-income groups, but among the broad masses of people they are no substitute for traditional religious values."

One may wonder why there is so little protest of truly religious people against this very widespread, but still quite arrogant argument. Be what it may, the argument itself is also self-defeating. Once you have to resort to it in order to defend religion, it becomes useless. If there is any "social usefulness" in religion, it would work best, if it is not consciously reflected upon. It would only work, if religion is still adhered to for its intrinsic values and spiritual content. <It is a little bit like if my little daughter would only eat her porridge because otherwise a huge green monster would come and devour her. Once I tell her that I have only invented this huge green monster for the good purpose of making her eat, it won't do anymore. Be assured that I don't educate my daughter this way>

Also the basic conflict between civil society and religion is not settled. Is really *every* traditional religion equally a supporting substructure for civil society? Are the various religions within one civil society always compatible or may they resort to violence (as they did in the age of the crusades) when they conflict with each other?

It takes the proper definition of the Lockean concept to settle some of these questions. Lockean natural rights-theories, as essentially very secularist concepts, are often accused of being "atomistic" and of undermining religion and morality. This inevitably puts the question of liberal secularism on the agenda. Although there has been a tendency in some countries with "secular" political systems (almost all of Western Europe) that, for instance, church attendance has been declining, it is a contradiction in itself that liberalism advocates a secular, if not "permissive" lifestyle. The aim of liberalism is to ensure an open process by protecting the unalienable rights. Hence it does not aim at the establishment of any particular "lifestyle". This may not sound too impressive for a religious-minded person, but the consequences of this very tolerant principle are more far-reaching than commonly supposed. The reason why this is so, is that most people have very inaccurate and prejudiced views of these consequences, into which they where led by some "false friends" of liberal secularism and some very non-liberal secularist governments especially in the Islamic world.

The first prejudice is that the advocates of immorality are the natural friends of tolerance. In the United State, for instance, the editor of a pornographic magazine called "Hustler" was hailed as a champion of tolerance and individual rights in a widely discussed movie a year ago, simply because broke with some moral taboos and somehow managed to make any moral censure of it (e.g. by the churches and other religious communities) look like an intolerant act that violated his rights to live like he wanted to live. This, of course, includes a gross misunderstanding of the basic principles of liberal secularism and civil society. Of course, a liberal must be against any form of coercion by government, that violates the right of a person to his property to which his personal views about pornography also belong. There must be no government censorship. But it also implies that within society there is a right to speak out about and to censure immoral tendencies in cultural life. It does not mean that a attack on taboos is per se an expression of liberalism. Liberty does not mean that nobody is allowed to tell you what you can or cannot do. Social ostracism and boycotts are, although it may not always serve good purposes, legitimate means, to ensure that moral and religious standards have a voice in society.

The second prejudice is that a secularist state has to enforce secularist standards upon all social sub-structures of a civil society. Among some Western intellectual circles this goes so far that people think that it would be a task of government to ensure and enforce a "pluralistic" approach on the Catholic Church and even non-catholics find it appropriate to protest against celibacy of catholic priests. When some weeks ago the arch-bishop of Cologne announced that the catholic church was not a democracy but a "christocracy", he was expressing a mere triviality. All Christian churches (and Islam, too) appeal to a higher divine law, that cannot be subjected to democratic decisions - otherwise they would cease to be religions at all. Nevertheless many politicians went to the press declaring that they were enraged about this announcement. In a halfway secular liberal country like Germany this fortunately remains without consequences. The Church is not forced to abjure its "christocratic" credo. In countries with a non-liberal secularist political system consequences may be harsher. Enforced secularism may even cause a backleash, like in Iran, toward an enforced religious fundamentalism.

A civil society is by definition a peaceful society that is not here to impose "its" views upon its citizens. It is important to know that it does not per se encourage "permissiveness" or prohibit specific social organisations with very concrete and exclusive moral or religious aims. Not "levelling" secularism is the standard of such a civil society, but the possiblity to pursue your own values within a framework of voluntary cooperation. Edmund Burke, who (as I mentioned above) saw religion as a pillar of civil society, was very well aware of this when in 1792 he claimed that churches were "voluntary societies". The fusion of civil society with religion can only work if the communal structures that support religion are thus "privatised". This may mean (depending on the concrete character of the religion) that a civil society may thwart some religious aspirations. If, like some forms of Islamic fundamentalism, a religion claim does claim to present a "higher law" and does not distinguish between state and society, a conflict may be inevitable. There may be a clash between two "higher laws" - the religious law and the natural rights of a secular civil society. However, what a civil society of the liberal type can guarantee is that the members of a religious community can organise themselves in an exclusive way. The outcome is not necessarily a "wishy-washy" secularised version of religion. In a free civil society they can (and, if they are serious about their believes, have to) be convinced that they are in possession of the ultimate truth, while all others are mere "infidels". They may try, although rarely succeed, to make their views the common consensus of society. More likely is the emergence of something different, for which here in this country the Ottoman Empire has provided us with one of the best examples - i.e. a society where different religious communities are allowed to run their own affairs by laws of their own choice. This model, although of medieval origin, still looks refreshingly modern and libertarian. It shows that undiluted religious conviction can cooexist with tolerance. What the principles of a civil society only demands, is that religious communities are, so to say, "disarmed" and allow the right to "exit".

Religious communities (like other special interest groups) must not instrumentalise government for their purposes, unless the purpose is the mere protection of their rights. After all, a genuine liberal secularism wants only to secularize politics, not the private sphere. Therefore the politics of privatisation, that is so characteristic of modern liberalism, may also turn into a means of preserving religious values.

This demands an enormous self-restraint - sometimes vitalised by constitutional mechanisms - for both, the religions and civil society itself. Both Religion and Secularism may turn into threats to civil society. One should, however, not be too pessimistic. The exaggerated theories of *Samuel Huntington's* "Clash of Civilizations" have made us often forget, that the dislike of violence against persons and their property is something of a common stock of most established types of morality - be they secular or religious. What we observe today is rather a "clash of small groups of fundamentalists" than a "clash of religions" or "clash of civilizations". Especially in the Islamic world, as American Middle East-Expert *Graham Fuller* has recently remarked, the alleged threat of religious fanaticism is often misused by non-liberal secular regimes who want to receive economic and military support from Western democracies - Western democracies that would otherwise feel only contempt for these regimes. Maybe Fuller is right, when he sums up the problem, that the friends of democracy have unfortunately managed to look like the foes of Muslims. This conflict, I believe, can be resolved by clear thinking about the foundations of modern civil society. Reasonableness should prevail. This is also what Voltaire may have had in mind back in 1748. Remember: "Is there something more venerable than an old abuse?", asks Setok the merchant, to which Voltaire's hero, Zadig, replies: "The power of reason is considerably older."

ISLAM IN TURKISH POLITICS:
TURKEY'S QUEST FOR DEMOCRACY
WITHOUT ISLAM

Mustafa Erdoğan[*]

Recent Turkish politics have witnessed an outstanding and unexpected triumph of political Islam. Under the leadership of Necmettin Erbakan, a senior politician of the Islamist cause, the pro-Islamist Welfare Party (Refah Partisi) emerged from the national elections of December 1995 as the largest party in parliament. After a six-month struggle, it came to power in June 1996 as the senior partner in a coalition government with Ciller's True Path Party (TPP) and with Erbakan as prime minister. Before that, in March 1994, Welfare Party (WP) won municipal elections in several large cities. These developments vexed the Turkey's secular establishment; at first they attempted to block Erbakan's efforts to form a government. That is why Erbakan's search for a coalition partner took six months.

After forming government, the military, who views itself as the main guardian of the secular "Kemalist" state, tended to become involved in daily politics in order to protect the secularist state from so-called Islamicist infiltrations. In fact, on February 28, 1997, the military-dominated National Security Council issued a decree that required curbs on Islamic minded political, social, cultural, and economic groups. In the end, the military's "supervision" of Erbakan's government resulted in its forced resignation in June 1997. Following this, the pressure on the

---

[*] *Professor of Constitutional Law, Hacettepe University, Ankara, Turkey.*

Islamist groups increased, with some secular leaders hoping for a "settling of accounts" with political Islam.

It is interesting that the rise of Islam in recent Turkish politics, particularly in the case of Welfare Party, was considered a surprising event by both Turkish and foreign scholars. Just as an "Islamic revival" after the Democrat Party's coming to power in 1950 meant (among other things) adopting a relatively liberal policy towards Islam, so today "Islamic fundamentalism" is on the agenda not only of political circles, but also of academics. As the Turkish state elite began to think how to handle this "threat" to the secular Republic, it felt ready to find a "scientific" treatment for this "disease". Some felt a need to address the issue of reconciling Islam and democracy. Consequently, the literature on political Islam in general, and the Welfare Party in particular, started to increase. Nevertheless one thing remained unchanged: the advance of Islam in Turkey has been considered an accidental, even pathological, phenomenon. In this article I want to examine this approach that sees pro-Islamic tendencies as an abnormality and try to introduce a better way to understand this phenomenon.

Paradigmatic Error

According to the dominant paradigm in Turkish scholarship with regard to Islamic case, the rise of Islam is an exceptional phenomenon that must have a reasonable explanation. The main task for Turkish social scientists is to reveal the real causes that helped political Islam emerge so that it would be possible to cope with it "scientifically". If it is possible to find out those factors, it could be possible to prevent the politicalization of Islam. This approach seems to be derived from the modernization theory and Kemalist doctrine, which presupposes that as modernization process advances religion will loose its social appeal. A typical

Turkish scholar heavily influenced by the positivist outlook sees religion in general and Islam in particular as a reactionary force, "some evil and irrational force of mere orthodoxy and blind tradition".[1] In his/her opinion, in a modern society there is no place for religious institutions. For this reason, all religious-inspired social movements are considered "fundamentalist". If some movements inspired by religion begin to appear in public and/or political sphere, then some unusual factors must have created this. From a sociological perspective and with special reference to modernization theory, it is argued that people thrown into the margins of metropolitan areas as a result of urbanization and migration to the cities experience "unfair" income distribution, a quest for identity or an escape to traditional values caused by the difficulty in adjusting to an urban way of life. According to Sabri Sayari,[2] "(a)s a result of social and economic changes, particularly through urbanization and emigration, growing numbers of Turks appear to have developed a sense of `homelessness' following the disintegration of communal solidarities."

Some scholars believe that the ascent of political Islam in Turkey was aided by foreign financial and/or ideological dinamics. Arab money in particular is seen as one of the main sources of support for Islamic social and political movements. For example, Birol Yeşilada maintains that "the flow of Saudi Arabian capital into the Turkish economy strengthened the power position of Islamic fundamentalists."[3] Another social scientist, Sencer Ayata, implies the same: The Islamic bourgeoisie who are, it is argued, the Turkish collaborators with international Islamic capital is politically significant "due to its finance of Islamist activities.'[4] Besides, Türker Alkan referred to Iran's "attempt to spot the next country to experience the convulsions of a resurgent and militant Islam" and its seeing Turkey is an appropriate target of this effort.[5]

Sometimes, the "exceptional" appearance of Islam in public and political realms is attributed to the government's favored conduct towards Islamic groups and activities: "Turgut Ozal... wanted to promote Islam in the country. Indeed, in forming the Motherland Party, he chose 'fundamentalists'[6] as partners in early 1980s. Ozal saw himself as the person who could promote fundamentalism in the country..."[7] Sencer Ayata makes a similar argument: A new social class "grew as a result of the conscious efforts of Islamicists in the Motherland party governments who provided the Islamicist bourgeoisie access to credit from official sources... many such firms benefited significantly from state directed patronage and these companies, in turn, financially backed Islamist movements."[8]

However, other scholars seem ready to understand the meaning of Islam's involving in politics and to give Muslims their due. For example, Nilufer Gole contends that, in response to excluding from public sphere as a result of "cultural shift' or "civilizational conversion" initiated by the state elite during Republican era, some Muslims engaged in a search for self identity. From this point of view, "Islamism is the formation of the Muslim subject and agency which has been excluded from modernist definition of civilization and history-making".[9] Serif Mardin calls attention to another relevant fact: The Republican state tried to dissolve traditional Ottoman-Islamic bonds and replace them by new institutions, thereby creating room for religious influence at the individual level.[10] Sabri Sayari also writes in a similar vein: "(T)he popularity of Islamic revivalist movements, religious orders, traditional Qur'anic principles and fundamentalist political movements, all of which hold the attraction of reintegrating the individual into a social order where Islam provides the basis for solidarity and identity."[11] Another aspect of Islamic movements, to which Binnaz Toprak (among others) refers, is that they try to get space for themselves in the status hierarchy of society.[12]

Alan R. Taylor's judgement seems to be fair one about the rise of Islam: "The moderate return to Islam in Turkey is not a resurgence but an attempt to redress an imbalance that was an integral part of the Kemalist system. It presents a desire of the Turkish people to create available synthesis of values and identities in which Islam is allowed to play a part without excluding other elements of national culture:"[13]

Democratization and Islamization

The prevailing paradigm in Turkish scholarship, which considers Islamization as an anomalous fact, is based on some incorrect presumptions. The underlying mistake is to see Islam as a strange factor, an outsider, to Turkish society and polity, a factor one has to ignore in any understanding and analyzing of modern Turkey. That is not all. Some scholars even see Islam as a "dangerous" phenomenon, a threat, and wish the state would suppress it as a societal force and an identity.

Islam, however, is a formative component of Turkey's social and cultural fabric. Historically and culturally, Turkey is a Muslim country, and most of the misunderstanding about Turkey's relationship to Islamic formations comes from the Kemalist elite's ignoring of this basic fact. By taking this history into account, Islam's visibility in public and political spheres is not a surprising phenomenon. In this context, what the Kemalist elite did not understand is that for Turkey Islam "is more than a doctrine, more than a private belief or worship. It is also a culture and ins titutional framework governing all aspects of interpersonal relations:"[14] For this reason it is not possible to consolidate democracy in Turkey by casting out Islamic factor and curbing Islamic political, social, economic and cultural movements.

As long as Islam is not suppressed by legal and political means, it necessarily will be reflected in Turkish politics and public debate. To put it differently, although the non-visibility of Islam in Turkish politics during early Republic (pre-1950) was the case, this was not because Islam had no societal basis but because it was not allowed to express itself publicly and politically. In this context, what is called the "rise of Islam", "Islamic revival", or "political Islam" is, in fact, simply suppressed Islam, which is embedded in Turkey's societal fabric, coming to the surface through the relative democratization of polity and "autonomization of civil society".[15] In other words democratization has led to the political participation of religiously conservative population and a raising of their demands, while autonomization of civil society has led to modernizing elite's "loos(ing) their power to transform the society from above:"[16] This potential had been kept under the Kemalist state's thumb until 1950, when the first free and competitive elections were held and the Democrat Party came to power. As pointed out by Sayari, "carried out in a heavy-hand fashion... Kemalist reforms created a good deal of hostility among the staunchly religious masses. When the same masses were given the chance to express their political preferences following the liberalization of the Turkish political system, Islam emerged as an important issue in the electoral mobilization of the largely peasant voters."[17]

During 1980s, a relatively pluralistic and free public debate developed, thanks partly to Ozal's liberal-conservative governments.[18] Islamic tendencies began to rise again both in societal and political levels. In this era the WP rose as "an institutional framework for the voiceless and suppressed masses of

Turkey and for social movements seeking redefine and transform social, cultural, and political interactions:"[19] However, Kemalist elite in both cases misunderstood this process and labeled it "reactionism" or "fundamentalism".

Some Notes On Republican History[20]

In order to understand better why the rise of Islam in Turkish politics has been getting stronger, one needs to have an idea about the political history of Republican Turkey. Contrary to the generally accepted view, Turkey, already had had an experience of constitutional government before the establishment of the republic in 1923. To an extent, a tradition of associational and political pluralism can be traced to the late nineteenth century. Both of this developments emerged from the Ottoman state's efforts to modernize its sociopolitical system in the post-Tanzimat (Reorganization) period with the imperial decrees known as the 1839 Gulhane Hatt-i Humayunu (the Royal Edict of Gulhane) and the 1856 Islahat Fermani (the Reform Edict). The first constitutional monarchy came after these measures, when Abdulhamit II put into force a semi-parliamentarian, monarchical constitution in 1876. Although the Sultan soon abrogated the constitution (1878), the Young Turks forced him to put the constitution into effect again in 1908, and in the following years the constitution was amended to conform to that of a Western-style parliamentary monarchy.

Despite official pressures between 1878-1908, associational life and constitutional movement had managed to survive. Immediately after "proclamation of freedom"[21] by the Young Turks, the number and activities of political, ethnic, cultural, and literary associations began to increase rapidly. In this period many associations and parties involved in public debate and political process.[22] Unfortunately, a 1913 military conspiracy led by the Unionists, whose ideology was based on a positivistic outlook, nationalism, and solidarism, stopped the democratic political process and attempted to oppress all opposition movements, whether Islamist, liberal, socialist, or ethnic civil groups. The First World War followed the capturing of late Ottoman polity by the Unionists, and the parliamentary process was interrupted until the end of 1919, when general elections for a House of Representatives (Meclis-i Mebusan) was held. However soon after the new Ottoman assembly began to operate, it had to end its work (April 1920) under pressure from the British forces occupying Istanbul. Subsequently, the Sultan dissolved it officially.

The closure of the parliament prompted the national-liberationist organizations of Anatolia, under the leadership of Mustafa Kemal, to initiate the Grand National Assembly (GNA) in Ankara on April 23, 1920. The declared purpose of GNA was to liberate the country and the sultan-caliph from the foreign occupiers' oppression. The main preoccupation of the GNA, in terms of its internal operation, was to claim exclusive authority over the "affairs of the nation", and, as a matter of fact, it showed much care about keeping democratic legitimacy, even though there existed an emergency situation because of the independence war. For this reason, the GNA could hardly passed an act that made Kemal the commander-in-chief of the nationalist forces, a power that was supposed to be part of the sovereign authority of the GNA itself.

Shortly after the ending of "national struggle", the way of doing things in politics began to change, and democratic concern for legitimacy and pluralism gradually was replaced by more autocratic methods initiated by M. Kemal and his close associates. The first step in this direction happened when a majority of this

GNA, under the influence of M. Kemal, passed an act for early elections in violation of provisions in the 192I Constitution. Held in summer of 1923, the elections resulted in the "cleansing" of the parliamentary opposition the "Second Group" (Ikinci Grup),[23] which consistently had resisted to M. Kemal's efforts to rule over the GNA. Thus, the GNA lost its representative-democratic feature, and this, in turn, made easier for M. Kemal and his close associates to manipulate the GNA's agenda and to dominate the policy of the nation. In this era, Kemalist ruling circle did not allow opposition groups to have a voice in Turkish polity. In fact, the first political challenge, that of Republican Progressive Party which alleged that Kemal was monopolizing political power and establishing an autocratic government,[24] came from some of M. Kemal's own friends, who had served with him during the war of liberation. But this party was banned by the government in 1925, only a few moths after its formation, and its leading figures were sentenced to life in prison following a court martial.

In 1930, M. Kemal asked his Iongtime and close friend, A. Fethi, to form an opposition party on liberal lines in order to criticize the government -but not the regime, state, or president, who was M. Kemal himself. However the new Free Republican Party dissolved itself in the same year, after it appeared that the partyt had the potential to gain a considerable electoral support, a situation that could challenge Kemal's Republican People's Party (RPP), especially in rural areas. Those experiments showed that "neither Ataturk personaly nor the Turkish potitical elites collectively were ready to proceed to a full-fledged multi party democracy".[25]

In time, the process of monopolization of the polity by M. Kemal and his ruling RPP was supplemented by invading all civil society domains. The 1925 Kurdish uprising,[26] which broke out in eastern Anatolia, provided the power elite with an excuse to suppress all the autonomous elements of society, especially ones whose aspiration came from religious belief. Indeed, after 1925 the Republican state gradually became an RPP apparatus to change radically the social and cultural fabric of the Turkish society in accordance with the RPP's blue-print for a secular-nationalist society and to create a new man, or, to coin a term, homo Kemalicus. For this reason, the free press was suppressed, the educational system was monopolized by the state (the Act of Unification of Education, 1924), pious endowments were brought under strict state control (1924), and all civic associations that had potential to remain autonomous from the state were banned or dissolved. Thus, dervish lodges were dissolved in 1925, the Turkish Hearths clubs were banned in 1931 and Turkish Association of Women was dissolved in 1935. To fill the cultural and moral void caused by pruning the civil and cultural formations, the government established a network of People's Houses. These were supposed to have an official mission of indoctrinating society along secularist-nationalist lines, that is, to provide the state with a cultural-ideological hegemony over the society. Moreover, as a part of the project to cut off all linkages of the society with traditional institutions and knowledge, a reform of higher education was introduced. A major aim of this reform was shutting down of the Darulfunun, the Ottoman university located in Istanbul.[27]

With the oppression of civil society, the authoritarian one-party government lasted until 1945, when the ending of Second World War started "the second wave of democracy" throughout the world and, in turn, created a favorable foreign milieu for Turkey to transform its system into a multiparty government. The ruling RPP, led by Ismet Inonu, heir to Kemal Ataturk as president, also decided to open up the political system in order to get popular support for its domestic program. Turkey then needed support from the Western world, especially from the United States, not only on account of its security problems with the Soviet Union but also on account of its bad economic situation. In order to handle the Soviet threat and to speed up economic recovery-Turkey's economy had been affected badly by the war even though it had not become involved in the conflict. It seemed to be a good decision to introduce competitive politics and to liberate the legal system. The 22 years of the one-party government had left a poor record, not only with respect to the economy but also in social and cultural terms. The general welfare level of the population, was barely above subsistence, except, of course, the growing class of big business, thanks to state support and wartime profiteering, and, to an extent, state officials. The oppression of civil and political activities, especially religious-inspired ones, had created a deep resentment and discontent among the rural population. In these conditions, there was a real need for the ruling elite to channel the widespread discontent into democratic institutions. Thus, the RPP allowed the social and political opposition to form parties and, the Democrat Party (DP) was established by some former RPP members, who had criticized policies of the government.

In the first free elections held in May 1950, the Democrat Party came to power, gaining a majority of seats in the parliament. However, although DP governments followed relatively liberal policies in terms of religious liberties and improved the general welfare of the population, its general record was far from the full liberalization and democratization and even was illiberal in some respects. Basically two reasons hindered genuine democratization. First, since the DP leaders came from the RPP tradition, their political career had been shaped by the RPP's authoritarian style of ruling. Second, while RPP paved the way to multiparty government, it was not really ready to cede control over the political system. It seems that Inonu and his close associates wanted to introduce "democracy" under the tutelage of the RPP, or a "limited democracy",[28] rather than a genuine competitive political system. In his project there were no place for giving up the ideological nature of the regime and allowing social forces to work according to their own dynamics. RPP leadership was certain that real power, in any case, would remain in their own hands in this new era because since the founding of the Republic the party had strengthened the system with ideological, legal, and institutional mechanisms and guaranties in favor of the Kemalist elite. Thus, DP governments were bound to operate within this limited or "contained" space.

In the post-1950 period, one of the most effective ways of containing democracy was to charge DP governments with favoring "reactionism" whenever liberal policies toward the religion initiated or whenever the exercising of civil rights by devout Muslims were tolerated. To make clear what RPP meant by the label "reactionism", the party accused the government of "endangering secularism", or fomenting an "uprising against the Republic" whenever religious people were allowed to enjoy the same liberties that were, and are supposed to be, usual in any Western democracy. The RPP charges culminated in military coup d'etat of May 27, 1960. The coup was led by army officers and supported by civil bureaucrats, intellecuals, and scholars who shared the same political outlook as RPP. Even though the DP had come to power by popular consent, the military junta retaliated and, in effect, returned political power back the pro-RPP state elite.

The new 1961 constitution appeared to be a liberal one, with guaranties for civil and political liberties and a strengthened judicial review. In some respects. however, it provided Kemalist state elite with the means of controlling over the political system by instituting procedures for the civil and military bureaucracy to check the decisions of elected bodies, which conservative parties were expected to control. The constitution also preserved the Kemalist ideological nature -secularism- of the regime. This new semi-liberal era again ended by military intervention in 1980. As a matter of fact, some liberal aspects of the constitution already had been trimmed in 1971-1973 period, when the political process operated under the military's supervision. The 1980 coup finally abrogated the constitutional order as a whole. The top generals pronounced one leading excuse for their intervention that the state again was endangered by "the escalation of reactionary activities" and "rising threat to secularism".

Between 1961-1980 Islam had began to gain visibility, not only in societal and cultural spheres, but also in the political realm, thanks to the new constitution's relatively liberal overtones which made it easier for the formerly oppressed religious groups to voice their demands. During this seemingly favorable atmosphere some Islamic-oriented politicians led by Necmettin Erbakan established the National Order Party (NOP) in 1969. However, the Constitutional Court disbanded the NOP in 1971 on the grounds of "capitalizing on Islam for political ends". The Court considered the NOP an anti-secularist party in terms of Turkish state creed of secularism, which means not just separation of religion and state, but also the state's domination over religion (Islam). In effect, the secular elite rejected granting civil and political liberties to the people who claimed to be inspired by the Islamic faith. This conception of democracy "has often excluded not only the radical but also moderate Islamists".[29] In other words, Erbakan and his associates were wrong to think that the regime's "liberal" orientation embraced the Islamists as well.

Erbakan's close associates reformed their party in 1972 under the name of the National Salvation Party (NSP). According to Ilkay Sunar and Binnaz Toprak,[30] in terms of its socioeconomic background, the party represented "the protest of those who wanted larger political and economic role in the expanding world of modernity." But NSP's rhetoric was pro-Islamic and, it seemed to be a religious-conservative party. What NSP really sought to do was to help religious people, who had been excluded from the public and political realms since early days of the Republic, to influence the political processes and to feel themselves insiders to the system, or real citizens. Although the electoral record of NSP during 1970s was not impressive; Kemalist intellectuals, scholars, and military saw it as intolerable party in a secularist system. Thus, the NSP was shut down by the military government in 1981 .

Following the military intervention, the military junta, institutionalized as the National Security Council (NSC), designed a "constitution", which came into effect in November 1982. The main preoccupation of the framers of the 1982 Constitution was to consolidate the secularist-Kemalist characteristic of the regime and to narrow the space for political competition and civil society. Therefore, the NSC was given constitutional status as the basic platform for the military to influence political process. The constitution also strictly narrowed the room for the social and political expression of religiously-inspired civic organizations. A series of Kemalist "Reform Laws" that aimed to protect the secularist nature of the regime were equipped with a status of inviolability. During 1982-1983, the NSC amended many basic laws related to the framework of the political system so as to facilitate military supervision over the political process. However, while the coup leaders meant to curb political Islam, in some respects they favored Islamic belief, with the hope of "create(ing) a more homogenous and less political Islamic community", and they considered Islam "a pacifying and submissive ideology preferable to the threat of communism".[31] At the same time, the coup leaders' action "indicates that the tendencies and preferences given a relatively free rein in the three decades following Menderes' assumption of power can no longer be suppressed or ignored by the official classes who stand guard over Ataturk's legacy".[32]

The 1980's were, in one respect, the years of Turgut Ozal, first as primeminister and later as president. Ozal, who had been one of the top bureaucrats during the governments of Suleyman Demirel in 1970s, formed Motherland Party in 1983 and came to power at the end of the same year. Although as prime minister Ozal's liberalism in terms of economic policies did not reflect in political realm in same degree, his concept of state was considerably liberal in terms of the goals of state and the relationship between individual and state, and he had a tolerant attitude toward Islam. These facts contributed to the development of civil-societal activities, especially among Islamists, in post-1984 years. During his presidency, Ozal challenged the official Kemalist ideals and introduced new issues to the public debate that up to his time had been considered forbidden subjects to discuss. For example, he questioned the appropriateness of the state having an ideology, of the military controlling the policy of nation and of the Kurdish policy followed by previous governments. Moreover, being a devout Muslim, Ozal helped to change the official hostile policy toward Islam and religious people and normalized access of religious people to civil service jobs. According to Taylor, "what seems to be most appealing to a large number of Turks is Ozal's ability to reaffirm his commitment to Islam in a secular setting with which he is comfortable."[33]

Shortly after Ozal's death in 1993, the political atmosphere started to change and the military, through the NSC, gradually reassumed the initiative in government policies. Thus, a policy of oppression concerning civil liberties, especially free debate and freedom of association, has increased. In this milieu, the members and the elected parliamentary deputies of the pro-Kurdish party, which represented Kurdish concerns in the parliament, were prosecuted and their party disbanded.

Another important event during these years was the rise of Islamic-minded Welfare Party (WP), which was organized in 1983 by some friends of Erbakan after the NSC permitted the formation of political parties. Interestingly, as the heir to the NSP of the pre-1980 period, WP had limited public appeal and little electoral success during Ozal's years. After Ozal's death, however, the party won the municipal elections held in March 1994. Subsequently, the WP received 21 percent of the vote cast in December 1995 parliamentary elections, a higher percent of votes than that obtained by any other political party.

Even though the WP held the largest number of seats in the parliament, it was not easy to find a coalition partner with which to form a government. The Kemalist-secularist sector (the military, professional organizations. academia, parties of the center, big media and some sections of the civil bureaucracy) argued that as an "anti-system" party, WP could not be a legitimate partner to any other "secular" party. However, the Motherland Party, led by Mesut Yilmaz, did try to form a coalition government with the WP but eventually gave up its initiative. After the fall of a short-lived Motherland-True Path Party (TPP) coalition, the WP at last managed to form a coalition with Ciller's conservative-populist TPP in the summer of 1996 despite the harsh criticisms of the media and other Kemalist circles. These criticisms grew during the course of the WP-TPP coalition government, and by early 1997 the military-dominated NSC began to involve itself actively in daily politics. To the top generals, who saw the army as prime guardian of the secularist Republic, the state of affairs was no longer tolerable. In February they issued a memorandum through the NSC that required the government basically to persecute so called reactionary organizations and activities.

In the end, the NSC forced government parties to resign in June 1997. The military's main target was WP, rather than the TPP. The generals' priority was to drive the WP from the office. This was the case, because "the system of values inculcated by the armed forces is deemed to be inseparable from Ataturk's conception of the secular state. When those ideals have been threatened, or public order threatens the stability of the Kemalist republic, senior military officials have felt it necessary to intervene."[34] The next step was to file a suit against the WP in the Constitutional Court, which ordered the disbanding of the party in January 1998. It might be worthwhile to note that, in this process, the big business and associated big media interests willingly supported the generals. Otherwise, it would not have been so easy to drive the WP out of the government. However, this does not mean that political Islam is excluded from Turkish politics permanently. As Atilla Yayla put it: "Refah is a sociological reality that cannot be made to disappear through legal bans because it is the political expression of a huge opposition movement."[35] But the Kemalist army officers had intervened directly in the political arena again, this time by using a "constitutional" platform, NSC.[36] Thus, now the military once more is planning to do what it considers an "easy" business, that is, "reestablishing democracy".[37]

Radical Secularization in Turkey

From outset, the Kemalist state had reacted severely to all pro-Islamic and civil organizations. Its attitude toward Islam

73

remained unchanged, albeit in a more moderate mode after the transition to multi-party government. The key reason for this, it seems, is the ideological orientation of the Republican state, which from the beginning has been unfavorable to Islam. The state viewed Islam as the principal cause of Turkey's underdeveloped status . In fact, in the first two decades of the Republic the power elite tried to destroy Islam and its culture as a force in Turkey. After transition to multi-party government, the Kemalist elite continued its hostility to Islam, and even in the so-called constitutional periods based on 1961 and 1982 constitutions did not give up that policy. In the view of Kemalists, all they did originated from the dictates of secularism. However, as Kedouire observed, Turkish secularism is different from the Western model: "(I)t is not the state of affairs encountered in modern European politics and usually described by the phrase 'a free church in a free state'.[38]

In order to understand this policy better, it would be useful to glance at D. E. Smith's account of secularization policies in the modern world. In his analysis,[39] there are four aspects of secularization in the modern state: polity-separation, polity-expansion, polity transvaluation, and polity-dominance. These can be considered as stages, although a given secularization process may or may not follow each stage. At the first stage, the polity is separated from religious ideologies and ecclesiastical structures. "Polity separation secularization involves the severance of connection... between religion and the polity.... Polity separation frequently results in the contraction of the polity, as the government ceases to perform traditional religious practices".[40] In the stage of polity expansion, the state begins to perform regulatory functions in the socioeconomic sphere that formerly were performed by religious structures. "Here the polity extends its jurisdictions into areas of social and economic life formerly regulated by religious structures. The polity expands its functions at the expense of religion."[41] Polity-transvaluation secularization, that is the third aspect or stage, involves the support or creation of secular political values. Through the polity-transvaluation secularization process the state provides secularization of political culture, of the basis of legitimacy, and of national identity.

According to Smith, while "these three aspects of secularization are universal in the development of modern polities over the past century and a half", only in profoundly religious societies do we see a more radical form of secularization attempted: "the dominance of polity over religious beliefs, practices, and ecclesiastical structures. This involves the expansion of the polity into what is recognized as the purely religious sphere in order to destroy or radically alter religion."[42] In other words, "polity-dominance secularization involves an open governmental attack on the religious basis of the general culture and the forcible imposition of a secular ideology on the political culture... In denying any autonomy to the religious sphere, the state operates on totalitarian premises, although its overall philosophy need not be explicitly totalitarian."[43]

In the Turkish case, Kemalist secularism rested not on the separation between religion and state but on government control over religion. According to Levent Köker, the state sought to replace the Islamic value system with a "scientific" one.[44] The Republican state followed the "polity-dominance", or radical secularization, pattern as Smith himself[45] and Turkish scholar Ilter Turan[46] have stated. With a number of radical reforms, which included abolishing Caliphate, outlawing the tarikats (Sufi lodges), omitting Islam from the Constitution as the state religion and replacing Islamic law with an adaptation of the Swiss civil code, secularizing and monopolizing education, abolishing religious and traditional dress, and replacing the Arabic alphabet with the Latin alphabet, the "Kemalist government systematically dismantled Islam as the institutional basis of Turkish life in 1920s and 1930s."[47] In this era, radical secularism became "one of the key principles of Ataturk's new state and religious expression came under strict goverment supervision and control;"[48] any autonomy to Islam was denied.

Radical secularization of Turkish politics originated with Kemalist ideology, which developed during the early Republic. The formation of Kemalism as an ideology seemed to be a complex phenomenon, influenced in part by nineteenth century positivism, which had much appeal to the Young Turks, of whom M. Kemal was one. Kemalism incorporates a positivistic vision of the Enlightenment and peculiarities that emerged from the project to create a new nation based on mainly secularist lines in place of a traditional Islamic society. This is why Kemalists "advocated social and political progress through a positivist pursuit of science, which it was hoped would replace God-centered politics with an enlightened public mind... (Therefore) the legislation enacted in the first two decades of the republic was designed to replace Islamic communalism with a new mode of social solidarity constructed along the lines of progress."[49] In their opinion, "any kind of preoccupation with Islam" was "irrational" and Islam was "the antonym of enlightenment."[50] Thus, a suspicious, even hostile, attitude toward religion, a strong belief in positive science as a means of progress, nationalism, and a strict commitment to secularization of politics shaped the ideology of the ruling Kemalist elite.

Turkish Secularism: A Political Religion?

Not content with just separating Islam from politics, M. Kemal also sought to remove Islam's power base in society and subordinate it to the state. For this reason, secularism was introduced as the main political doctrine early in republic. In fact, the process of secularization of Turkish polity resembles the formation of "political religion". The term "political religion" was coined by David Apter, who observed: "States with monolithic structure, autocratic government and a wide range of community imperatives face a particular political problem" which results all social life being politicized in some degree. "When social life is heavily politicized, government requires exceptional authority. Such authority tends to be monopolistic. Monopolistic authority needs to replace older belief about other forms of allegiance. Now political forms are developed that have the effect of providing for the continuity, meaning, and purpose of an individual's actions. The result is a political doctrine that is in effect a political religion. The effects of political religion are such that they strengthen authority in the state and weaken the flexibility of the society."[51]

In a society in which a political religion prevails, "oppression obliterates freedom, fear replaces spontaneity, and everything is politicized, from family and kinship to voluntary associations."[52] In such cases "(h)armony in the political sphere derives from the messianic leader who points out the dangers and noxious poisons of faction. Many such leaders are charismatic who represent the 'one'. They personify the monistic quality of the system. To achieve such oneness, mobilization systems begin by politicizing all political life. As a result, politics as such disappears. This is in keeping with monistic political belief. Conflict is not only bad but also counterrevolutionary. It runs counter to the natural evolution of human society, and ideas of opposition downgrade and confuse the power of positive thinking. Ideas not only are dangerous, challenging the legitimacy of the regime or charisma of the leader. They also represent unscientific vestige wherever they run counter to those of the regime."[53]

Christel Lane, who studied political religion in the Soviet case, called our attention to the differences between political religion and civil religion.[54] First, civil religion links the political order with a transcendent power derived from the traditional religion of the society, whereas political religion presents a sacralization of the existing political order. Second, while civil religion confines itself to the political affairs of a society, political religion claims authority over all social life. "Consequently, political religion has a system of specific values and norms while the content of civil religion is at such a high level of generality that it conflicts neither with conventional religious nor with political norms and values."[55] The distinction becomes more clear when we turn to C. B. Bryant, who says:[56] "Society is the prime mover of the civil religion; the state is the prime mover of political religion. The collective representations in a civil religion are genuinely representative of society as a whole, or at least of many sections of it (...) By contrast, the collective representations of a political religion are superimposed on society by those who control the state. The one is historically rooted; the other is politically contrived. Alternatively, with civil religions it is ultimately the state which heeds society; with political religions it is ultimately society which submits to the state."

So, we can find most elements of political religion in Kemalist secularism and this fact made the early Republican regime closer to totalitarianism. In fact, Republican state was built in the form of monolithic structure, and had an autocratic government until 1950. Formerly M. Kemal and later Inonu, with the help of the RPP apparatus, monopolized political power and eliminated factual and potential rivals. In Kedourie's words,[57] "(Republican) People's Party was meant by its founder (that is, M. Kemal) to be an instrument for the political control of the masses, and as a transmission-belt, auxiliary to the administration, the purpose of which was to promote Mustafa Kemal's secularist project." The RPP was not of the kind of party that we see in Western constitutional and representative democracies, but an apparatus through which the population could be indoctrinated into Kemalist outlook, secularism being most prominent in it. In order to mobilize the masses, in addition to the party apparatus, People's Houses were established and they were supposed to work in the same direction, and, as a matter of fact, they did so.

The Kemalists also had charismatic leaders, Kemal Ataturk himself, and later Inonu, even though the latter never enjoyed the same degree of respect and authority as did Ataturk, who represented the "one" and personified the monistic character of the regime. Indeed, from 1922 M. Kemal, "who was like a sultan",[58] had been called officially "Gazi". Although that title refers to any man who fought for a holy cause in the context of Islamic culture, in this case it implied that M. Kemal was the Gazi. not just one of many Gazis. In 1934, the Grand National Assembly, which then was controlled by M. Kemal's RPP, gave him the surname Ataturk, which means `the ancestral father of Turks". And M. Kemal's charisma was propagated and strengthened through the educational mechanisms, the press that was under strict control of the government, and in many ceremonial occasions.

Another interesting similarity to the political system with political religion is that conflict was considered heretical, "not only bad but also counterrevolutionary" in the Kemalist ideological context. During the single-ruling-party period, any opposition to the Kemalist tenets, in terms of ideas or actions, regardless of their Islamic, Kurdish, liberal, or socialist origins, was regarded as "unscientific", "subversive", or "reactionary". To the ruling elite, challenging Kemalism and the "draconian methods"[59] that were used by the government to consolidate secularist policies was challenging the national goal of "rising to the level of contemporary civilization", and disclosing the intention of making the society go back to the "darkness of the Middle Ages".

However, for any ruling elite, political religion could not be an end in itself. The final objective of creating a political religion is to incorporate a new value system and code of conduct-a civil religion to replace traditional religion. The term, but not the idea, of civil religion is a modern one, coined by Jean Jacques Rousseau in eighteenth century. In his account, civil religion refers to a distinction between "the religion of man" a s a private matter and the "religion of citizen" with its public connotations. However, the term was given contemporary currency with Robert N. Bellah's works, "Civil Religion in America"(1967) and *The Broken Covenant: American Civil Religion in Time of Trial* (1975). By civil religion Bellah refers to "that religious dimension, found... in the life of every people through which it interprets its historical experience in the light of transcendent reality."[60] According to J. A. Coleman, civil religion is "a set of beliefs, rites and symbols which relates a man's role as citizen and his society's place in space, time and history to the conditions of ultimate existence and meaning".[61]

In the case of Turkey, it seems that the long-term goal of the Kemalist elite was to replace Islam with a new civil religion that was to grow up from secular ideas and institutions. In designing a political religion such as Kemalism, the elite tried to make a secularist outlook and values rooted in the fabric of society, and this was expected to become the basis of new citizenship and public morality. M. Kemal tried to replace religion with a modernsecular ideology and the values of Republican nationalism and that ideology "came to constitute a 'civic religion' (with its public ritual to an extent that Islam probably never did under the Ottomans,"[62] The new system of secular norms, says Şerif Mardin, were to serve as a civic bond that was supposed to fill society's "ethical vacuum", which resulted from eliminating the traditional religious norms and to bring and keep the citizenry together as a political society.[63] Thus, a new mode of social solidariaty would replace "Islamic communalism".[64] In this context, what Heper called "to socialize the people into becoming patriotic citizens of a secular republic"[65] was, in fact, this very process of creating a civil religion. In this regard Kemalism resembles the French Revolution which, according to Bellah, "was anticlerical to the core and attempted to set up an anti-Christian civil religion".[66]

Though Republican state's efforts to replace Islamic-inspired traditional culture with a secular civil religion, Islam did not loose its appeal to the Turkish society at large. As a matter of fact, Islam is still the main basis of social solidarity, of mobilizing people for national goals, and an important source of legitimacy in politics. Therefore, making reference to Islam in Turkish politics is not, as Kemalists think of it, an indication of a conspiracy to "use" religion for political purposes. Perhaps, as Mardin pointed out,[67] Turkish Islam, which has been influenced by the general secularization, is going to transfer into a civil religion.

Conclusion

If it is true that Islam has penetrated Turkish social fabric deeply, has shaped interpersonal relations and an individual's conduct, and has remained the main reference for Turks in terms of the meaning of life, then it is not surprising that Islam has been able to find spaces for itself in Turkish social, cultural, public, and political life. Not only as a religious faith, but also as a code of conduct for individual and public concerns. Islam is embedded in Turkish society. If one considers Islam to be an outsider, then he fails to understand what is really happening in Turkish society and polity. And any ruling group that treats Islam as a stranger would be surprised to see Islam continue to grow consistently and must be ready to use force if it wants to suppress it. The Republican history shows that it is imposible to undermine lslamic social base and Islam's overall appeal to the population. By contrast, any attempt to suppress social and political movements motivated by Islamic concerns would lead to increased fundamentalist inclinations among Muslims.

Moreover, there is no strangeness in the growth of Islamization during democratization periods. If this process means a widening of the base of participation, with guarantied civil and political liberties, certainly, democratization would enable the citizenry, including devout Muslims, to express their demands and make their access to public debate and polity easier. Since the transition to competitive politics in 1946, this has been the case in Turkey. But the Kemalist elite considered this trend a counter-secularist uprising and reacted to it by force, as in 1960, 1971, 1980 and finally 1997. However, it is not a wise policy to apply the politics of coercion in response to social dynamics, rather than allowing these dinamics to express themselves politically.

Finally, an important point what Kemalists have overlooked is that many citizens always will see Islam as a source of knowledge, inspiration, guidance and action, even as a valuable way of life. This, in turn, will necessarily be reflected in the public and political spheres. Some people might define themselves through religious belief and choose Islam as a system of values to govern their lives. This is not a pathological phenomenon, as Kemalists seem to assume. As long as it allows things to operate in natural ways and is not tempted to exercise violence, the state is not fated to see such things as "fundamentalism", or a "reactionary threat". Turkey's political elite has to learn to live with Islam. If

Turkey really wants to be a democracy, it will do so successfully only with Islam, not by attempting to cast it off. Indeed, its history forces Turkey to be a "Muslim democracy". Labeling any Islamic minded movement as "fundamentalism" is not only a false diagnosis of the state of affairs in Turkey, but also a fatal act that would destroy the chance for democracy in Turkey, as Republican history showed so far.

Notes

I. Nur Yalman, "Islamic Reform and the Mystic Tradition in Eastern Turkey", *Archives Europeennes de Sociologie*, 10, 1969. p. 47; quoted in Richard Tapper, "Introduction", in Richard Tapper (ed.), *Islam in Modern Turkey: Religion, Politics and Literature in a Secular State* (London: I.B. Touris & Co Ltd: 1991). p. 7.

2. Sabri Sayari. "Politization of Islamic Re-traditionalism: Some Preliminary Notes", in Metin Heper & R. Israeli (eds.). *Islam and Politics in the Modern Middle East* (New York: St. Martin's Press, 1984), p. 25.

3. Birol Yesilada. "Turkish Foreign Policy Toward the Middle East", in A.Eralp & M.Tunay & B. Yesilada (eds.), *The Potitical and Socioeconomic Transformation of Turkey* (Westpoint, CT: Praeger Publishers. 1993), p. 189.

4. Sencer Ayata. "The Rise of Islamic Fundamentalism and its Institutional Framework", in *ibid.*, pp. 58-9. In another occasion. he writes: "The flow of capital from the Gulf States was used to found new banks to finance primarily investments undertaken by people in Naksibendi circles." See Sencer Ayata, "Traditional Sufi Orders on the Periphery: Kadiri and Naksibendi Islam in Konya and Trabzon", in R. Tapper (ed.). *op. cit.*, p. 224. For a similar view, see Ali L. Karaosmanoglu. "The Limits of Intemational Influence for Democratization'. Metin Heper & Ahmet Evin (eds.), *The Politics in the Third Turkish Republic* (Boulder/USA & Oxford/UK, 1994), p. 124).

83

5. Turker Alkan. "The National Salvation Party in Turkey". in M. Heper & R. Israeli, *op. cit.*, p. 79.

6. Yesilada does not need to differentiate between pious-conservative people and genuinely fundamentalists. In his writing, conservative means fundamentalist. However, Binnaz Toprak seems to be more meticulous in using terms: "(M)ajority of those who are categorized as Islamic fundamentalists are in a misplaced category if what is meant by fundamentalism is radical politics." See Binnaz Toprak, "Islam and the Secular State in Turkey", in Cigdem Balim & Ersin Kalaycioglu & Cevat Karatas & Gareth Winrow & Feroz Yasamee (eds.), *Turkey: Political, Social and Economic Challenges in the 1990s* (Leiden: E. J. Brill, 1995), p.95.

7. Birol Yesilada, *op. cit.*, p. 189, 178, 179.

8. Sencer Ayata, "The Rise of Islamic Fundamentalism...", p.58.

9. Nilufer Gole, "Authoritarian Secularism and Islamist Politics: The Case of Turkey", in Augustus Richard Norton (ed.), *Civil Society in the Middle East*, v. 2 (Leiden: E. J. Brill, 1996). pp. 21-26.

10. Serif Mardin," The Naksibendi Order in Turkish History". in Tapper (ed.). *op. cit*, p. 139.

11. Sabri Sayari. *op. cit.*. 123.

12. Binnaz Toprak. *op. cit.*. p. 95.

13. Alan R. Taylor, *The Islamic Question in the Middle East Politics* (Boulder and London: Westview Press, 1988), p. 91 .

14. Alan R. Taylor. *ibid*. p. 32.

15. M. Hakan Yavuz called this fact "normalization of state-society relations". See his article. "The Return of Islam: New Dynamics in State-Society Relations and the Role of Islam in Turkish Politics", in *Turkey: The Pendulum Swings Back* (London: Islamic World Report. 1996), p. 79.

16. Nilufer Gole, "Toward an Autonomization of Politics and Civil Society in Turkey", in M. Heper & A. Evin, *op. cit.*, p. 222.

17. Sabri Sayari, *op. cit.* p. 126.

18. For more information about Ozal's place in Turkish politics, see my book *Demokrasi, Laiklik, Resmi İdeoloji* (Democracy, Secularism and the State Ideology) (Ankara: LDT Yayınları, 1995), pp. 1 18-130.

19. See M. Hakan Yavuz. "Political Islam and Welfare (Refah) Party in Turkey", *Comparative Politics*, v. 30 (October 1997), P. 74.

20. This section is based mainly on my book, *Türkiye'de Anayasalar ve Siyaset* (Constitutions and Politics in Turkey) (Ankara: Liberte, 1999).

21. "Hürriyetin İlanı". This term was popular during the second constitutional era of Turkey.

22. Authors who emphasize the lack of civil society in Ottoman empire fail to consider this point. For an example, see Ali Kazancigil, "The Ottoman-Turkish State and Kemalism", in Ali Kazancigil & Ergun Ozbudun (eds.), *Ataturk: Founder of a Modern State* (Hamden/CY: Archan Books, 1981), p. 45.

23. On the Second Group in GNA see Ahmet Demirel, *Birinci Mecliste İkinci Grup* (The Second Group in The First GNA) (Istanbul: Iletisim, 1995).

24. Elie Kedourie, *Politics in the Middle East* (Oxford: Oxford University Press, 1992), p.108; Erik Jan Zurcher. Turkey: *A Modern History* (London: I. B. Tauris and Co Ltd. rev. paperback ed., 1997). p. 176.

25. Dankwart Rostow. "Ataturk as an Institution-builder", in A. Kazancigil & E. Ozbudun, *op. cit.,* p. 74.

26. Being a Muslim people and an active participant in liberation war, Kurds were assumed to be one of the founding peoples of the new state, the other being Turks.

27. Given this state of affairs, it is surprising that Heper writes as follows: "From 1923, when the republic was founded, until the mid-1940s, democracy itself gradually established". See. Metin Heper, "Islam and Democracy in Turkey: Toward a Reconciliation", *The Middle East Journal*, V. 51 (Winter 1997). p. 33.

28. Kemal Karpat, *Turkey's Politics: The Transition to a Multi-Party System* (Princeton, NC: Princeton University Press, 1959). p. 147.

29. Metin Heper, *op. cit*, p. 45.

30. Ilkay Sunar & Binnaz Toprak, "Islam in Politics: The Case of Turkey", *Government and Opposition*, n.18, (Autumn 1983), p. 438.

31 . Hakan Yavuz, "Political Islam..:', p. 67.

32. Kedourie, *op. cit.*. p. 148. According to another reading, "that approach which was adopted is an effort to overcome the serious division that then characterized Turkish society and had Ieft more than 5.000 people dead and 20.000 injured from 1977-1980. A combination of religion and nationalism was perceived as a means of linking both the moderate right and left wings of the Turkish political spectrum." See Ben Lombardi, "Turkey: The Return of the Reluctant Generals?", *Political Science Quarterly*, v, 112, n. 2 (Summer 1997), p. I96.

33. Alan Taylor, *op. cit.*, p. 91 .

34. Lombardi, *op. cit.*, p. 209.

35. Atilla Yayla, "Erbakan's Goals", *Middle East Quarterly*, v. 4, n. 3 (September 1997). p. 25.

36. A foreign observer wrote in mid -1996: "All seem to be setting the stage for a return to military rule." See, Lombardi, *op. cit.,* p. 213.

37. Ernest Gellner gives such a nice sketch as follows: "I think it was Mark Twain who said. 'Giving up smoking is easy, I 've done it so many times." The Turkish army could say,

'Reestablishing democracy is easy, we have done it so many times." See his article "The Turkish Option in Comparative Perspective", in Sibel Bozdogan & Resat Kasaba (eds.), *Rethinking Modernity and National Identity in Turkey* (Seattle and London: University of Washington Press, 1997), p. 243. For a more detailed account of the Turkish politics during the years of 1995-1997, see my book, *Rejim Sorunu* (The Regime Question) (Ankara: Vadi Yayinlari. 1997).

38. Elie Kedourie, *op. cit.,* pp. 105-106.

39. Donald Eugene Smith, *Religion and Political Development* (Boston: Little Brown and Company. 1970), pp, 85-123.

40. *Ibid.,* p. 91 .

41. *Ibid.,* pp. 96-97.

42. *Ibid.,* p. 85, 86.

43. *Ibid.,* p. 119.

44. See Levent Koker, *Modernlesme, Kemalizm ve Demokrasi* (Modernization, Kemalism and Democracy) (Istanbul: lletisim, 3rd rep. 1995), p. 166, 168, 224.

45. Smith, *op. cit.,* p. 86, 118, 121,268:

46. Ilter Turan, "Religion and Political Culture in Turkey", in Tapper (ed.), *op. cit.,* p. 34. "The Turkish state was the most radical example of modern secularization. The republic of Ataturk was found on nationalist and republican principles and undertook a veritable cultural revolution to liquidate the attachment of the Turkish people to their Islamic past." See Ira M. Lapidus, "The Golden Age: The Political Concepts of Islam", in Charles Butterworth & l. William Zartman (eds.), *The Annals: Political lslam* (Newbury Park: Sage Publications, 1992), p. 21 .

47. See Taylor. *op. cit.,* p. 31. Another (Turkish) scholar gives an overall account of the measures that were meant to sweep religious inspirations away from Turkish socio-cultural and political lives: "the abolition of Caliphate (...); the abolition of the

office of the Seyhul-Islam, the highest in the religious hierarchy of the Ottoman Empire(...); the abolition of the medreses, the Islamic educational institutions for higher learning; and the secularization of the educational system; the abolition of the religious courts and the secularization of the legal system; the outlawing of the mystical Sufi brotherhoods, the tarikat(...). and the closing of their places of worship and gathering: (...) the outlawing of the veil for women working in civil service jobs; the change in official oath, to be taken on one's honour rather than on the Koran; the change of weekly holiday from Friday to Sunday; the adoption of the Latin alphabet instead of the Arabic; and the abolition of the Muslim lunar calendar in favour of the Gregorian. At the same time, a scries of laws were implemented to prevent an organized political movement based on Islam:' See Binnaz Toprak, *op. cit.,* p. 91 . See also Richard Tapper, *op. cit.,* p. 2

48. Richard Tapper, *ibid.*

49. Faruk Birtek. "Prospects for a New Center or the Temporary Rise of Peripheral Asabiyah?", in M. Heper & A. Evin (eds.), *op. cit.,* p. 224.

50. Metin Heper, *op. cit.,* p. 42.

51. David E. Apter, "Political Religion in the New Nations", in Clifford Quest (ed.), *Old Societies and New States: The Qtrest for Modernity in Asia and Africa* (New York: The Free Press of Glencoe. 1963). pp. 58-59.

52. *Ibid.,* p. 68.

53. *Ibid.,* p. 78.

54. Christel Lane. *The Rites of Rulers: Ritual in Industrial Society- the Soviet Case* (Cambridge: Cambridge University Press, 1981), p. 42.

55. *Ibid.*

56. Christopher G. A. Bryant; "Civic Nation, Civil Society. Civil Religion", in John A. Hall (ed.), *Civil Society: Theory, History Comparisons* (Cambridge: Polity Press, 1995), p. 150.

57. Elie Kedourie, *op. cit.*. pp. 107-108.

58. *Ibid.*, p. 108.

59. *Ibid.*, p. 106, 108. Lombardi called those methods "Ataturk's brutal repression of religion". See Lombardi. *op. cit.*, p. 197.

60. Robert Bellah, "Civil Religion in Amecica", Daedalus , v. 96 (1967), p. 13. "Rather than Anglo-Saxon liberalism. French lacobinism, with its highly centralized model of change, became the prototype for reform of Turkish modenists. Hence, secularization itself became part of that process of social engineering rather than an outcome of the process of modernization and societal development" See Nilufer Gole, "Secularism and Islamism in Turkey: The Making of Elites and Counter-Elites", *The Middle East Journal*, v. 51 . n. I (Winter 1997), p. 48.

61. Cited in Bryant, *op. cit.*, p. 49.

62. Richard Tapper, *op. cit.*. pp. 5-7.

63. Şerif Mardin, "Religion and Politics in Turkey". in James P. Piscatori (ed.). *Islam in the Political Process* (Cambridge: Cambridge University Press. 1983). p. 142. 156.

64. Faruk Birtek, *op. cit.*. p. 224.

65. "By means of the mass media, education, flag saluting, national anthem singing, state parades and nonreligious holidays on national anniversaries, attempts were made to socialize the people into becoming patriotic citizens of a secular republic rather than pious members of a Muslim community" See Metin Heper, *op. cit.*. p. 3:1.

66. Robert N. Bellah, *The Broken Covenant* (New York: The Seabury Press, I975). p. 3.

67. Serif Mardin, "Islam in Mass Society: Harmony Versus Polarization", M. Heper & A. Evin (eds.), *op. Cit.*, pp. 167-68.

ISLAM, DEMOCRACY AND TURKEY

Ahmet Aslan[*]

The rulers and intellectuals of Muslim societies have long debated and discussed the compatibility between Islam and democracy. It is generally accepted that the problems generated by this relationship also constitute a major issue to be tackled in the modernisation projects and programmes of Muslim countries.

The answers given and positions taken about the relationship fall into two or three different categories. Since the last century, during which the first serious intellectual-cultural contacts with the Western world began, some Muslim leaders and intellectuals have been suggesting that democracy, along with other similar concepts of the modern world such as constitutional administration, secularism and human rights, are not incongruous with the basic values and notions of Islamic civilisation. They claim, in fact, that these concepts are in complete harmony with it. Some groups and individuals, surfacing over the last fifty years, have asserted quite the opposite. They argued, at first with a certain shyness, lately with more self-confidence, that those concepts and institutions rooted in the West, chief among them democracy, have no place in the religion of Islam, in Islamic culture and Islamic traditions. They hold the view that democracy itself is a concept that is incompatible with Islam. Among the individuals and groups making this case one can cite Sayyid Qutb, the famous theorist of the Muslim Brotherhood; Abu'l Ala Mawdudi, the renowned ideologist of the Pakistani group of Jamaat-i Islam; another famous Islamist, the Iranian intellectual Ali Shariati; the Islamic Salvation

---

[*] *Professor of Philosophy, Aegean University, Izmir, Turkey.*

91

Front which has challenged the regime in Algeria; and Ali Bulaç, who is an example of those expressing similar opinions in Turkey.

The arguments

The main arguments and theses that the representatives of the former position put forth in connection with the relations between Islam and democracy may be summarised as follows; During the period of the four caliphs, a period representing the golden age of the Islamic state, the rulers came to power through elections. A mechanism relying on the consent of the community was adopted for the first Muslim caliphs to be charged as leaders. In Islam, there are three main guides used to determine the principles to be followed in societal administration and in the organisation of relations between individuals: the Koran, the Sunna (sayings and doings of the Prophet) and the Ijma. This latter represents a consensus, a compromise first among the scholars who have the authority to interpret the religion accurately and then among all Muslims. Also, one of the most important principles of Islam is that there are certain individuals – the ulema (theologians) and the faqih (Islamic judges) –who are invested with the authority to formulate the rules relating to the problems which may arise in the social life of Muslims. These decisions must take into consideration the interests of society or general interest. This is the principle of maslahat. Furthermore, the principle of separation of powers is also found in Islam.

Besides these, the presence of some other essentially democratic principles in Islam are highlighted. For instance, as everyone knows and as Gellner draws particular attention to, one of the most important characteristics of high Islamic culture is the absence of an institution such as a church to mediate between God and man; Islam's basic egalitarian attitude which opposes every kind of hierarchy is considered to be one of these democratic principles. Additionally, Islam attaches no importance to race, nationality, wealth or poverty and class. This kind of non-discriminatory individuation fits in well with a democratic climate. The legal equality recognised by Islam for everyone irrespective of social position and class distinction is also evaluated as an element which best projects a democratic mentality.

On the other hand, those who oppose this view of good relations and theoretical harmony between Islam and democracy are quick to note other aspects of Islam. They contend that Islam does not distinguish between the religious community and political community. In other words, they remind us that Islam did not establish a careful balance between the realm of Caesar, the temporal ruler, and the realm of God. Moreover, they emphasise that Islam imposes the Shari'a as law and as the constitution, and does not allow men to make laws for themselves, by themselves. The recognition of the Shari'a as the foundational law gives those religious scholars who have the authority to interpret it, a distinct and decisive role in approving or refusing governmental policies. This is also seen as an element incongruous with the basic idea or theory of democracy.

There are, apart from the above, more particular handicaps. For instance, in terms of legal status, Islam does not recognise equality between genders or between Muslims and non-Muslims. The case, in terms of political participation, is more ambiguous. Parallel to this, Islamic tradition refuses the appointment of women and non-Muslims to executive, administrative and judicial positions, although there is no clear reference to this in the Koran. This is also a practice that is incompatible with the recognised contemporary norms of democracy.

Perhaps more importantly, it is argued that the absolutist mentality of Islam in relation to politics is diametrically opposed to the relativist notion of viewing politics as a consequence of accommodation between wilful participants. This argument refers back to a very important and profound discussion, about whether or not the will of the people is also the will of God. Using the arguments of like-minded Christian theologians, leading Muslim intellectuals and writers criticise the democratic decision-making mechanism, as being no more than the sum of the arbitrary wills of individuals. For them, such a process does not concern itself with the pursuit of absolute truth.

A reality check on these multi-dimensional discussions carried out on the theoretical plane should constitute another important dimension of the relation between Islam and democracy. A group of scholars, among them most notably Samuel Huntington, cite actual experiences with democracy in Islamic countries. Huntington, evaluating the empirical evidence, draws attention to the fact that the only country among Islamic countries that sustains a democratic political system is Turkey. He also points out, as an equally pertinent fact, that democracy in Turkey is not based on Islam, nor does it define itself by Islamic references. Rather, democracy in Turkey is institutionalised despite Islam and because it took the risk of a rupture with Islam. In short, scholars argue that the relations between Islam and democracy are not harmonious in practice, irrespective of the theoretical niceties in debates. Huntington also reminds his readers that opposition movements in Islamic countries usually betray a fundamentalist character, and those movements that seek a democratic order are relatively weak.

In fact, we must agree that, in practice, democratic development in Islamic countries are double- edged. In almost all

Islamic countries, opposition movements, carry the banners of democracy, human rights, and democratic values while they oppose existing despotic, autocratic regimes. On the other hand, enough signs exist to show that these movements or their spokesmen are not committed to democracy as a positive doctrine and a positive program.

To illustrate the point we can use some examples from Turkey. The mayor of Istanbul, a leading representative of the Islamist Welfare Party (WP) once stated that he sees democracy as just a means to reach a treasured end (Islamic rule), much as a trolley to be taken to one's final destination. We can also recall that Mr. Necmettin Erbakan often reflected on that quality of democracy that exalts the will of the majority since this was a principle that served his interests, But in his various declarations and acts, Mr. Erbakan, the chairman of the WP, displayed an almost total lack of sensitivity about the personal rights and freedoms of minority groups or individuals that are equally as important as majority rule.

Another important area for research in this context would be the attitudes of the common people toward the practice of democracy in Islamic countries. It is absolutely necessary to note the appreciation of democracy that one finds among a majority of ordinary citizens when they are given the opportunity to express themselves. This attitude, which necessarily ignores the questions of whether democracy is or is not congruent with the theory, history, culture and traditions of Islam, is highly encouraging for those individuals who appreciate or who believe in democracy, since the transition to democracy in Turkey over fifty years ago, no evidence has emerged that the people think that democracy is antithetical to Islamic theory and Islamic traditions. Nor is there any sign that they took democracy as something alien and incompatible with their beliefs, as something imported. To put it more simply, there is no serious indication that people are unhappy with the system of democracy, its practices, and its consequences. On the contrary, there is plenty of evidence that the majority sees the general will as the most effective and useful institution for arranging their life as they wish and as their interests require. Ordinary Turks who are aware that political power is also their ticket to economic empowerment generally believe that the legitimacy of an administration depends on the people's vote obtained through free, competitive elections.

The Turkish experience

Turkey's history during the last 150 years presents a successful example of the encounter between Western and Eastern civilisations. This has been the period when a society belonging to the Muslim cultural world has encountered those institutions, values and concepts that have sprung up in the western world. During this period, a successful effort has been made to adopt and internalise attributes of the Western civilisation. This has been a regular and stable process, despite some interruptions from time to time, stretching from the Tanzimat (Reform Movement) in 1839 to Meşrutiyet (Constitutional Government) first in 1876 and then in 1908, to the Republic in 1923, and from the Republic to Democratisation in 1946. In this context, developments that have taken place in Turkey during the last ten to fifteen years should be viewed as the deepening of the Westernisation process which is penetrating a wider social strata rather than a regression from the achievements of that particular journey.

What exactly are the developments that have taken place in Turkey during the last ten to fifteen year? Economically, there has been a greater acceleration in the industrialisation process as manufacturing spread countrywide and led to the rise of peripheral actors. Small and medium enterprises have emerged as economic agents to be reckoned with, freedom of trade has expanded, the country has opened itself to the world markets, partaking in the globalisation process. The social changes accompanying these economic changes include an urbanisation process which is accelerating every day, with a rush from the periphery to the centre. The most remarkable development in the cultural domain is the shaping of a more pluralist, more polyphonic intellectual atmosphere going in tandem with the development of educational and communicational facilities and instruments. In Turkey, the development of a civil society that began with the transition to democracy has especially accelerated since the 1980's. The liberalising policies implemented by the late PM (then President) Turgut Özal in the economy, together with the enormous advances in communication, have created the basis for a more liberal, and thus a more democratic evolution in the intellectual domain as well.

Naturally, the new liberal and democratic developments have provided fertile ground for the Islamic movements that have been wishing to express themselves more freely and in a more institutionalised form since the transition to democracy. The most important consequence of this in the political domain has been the continual and regular advances that the Islamist Welfare Party (hereafter WP) has secured in the electoral front especially in the '90s. This growth allowed the party to emerge from the elections in December 1995 as the largest party and to finally attain power.

The 1980s were a period when the Islamic movement was ushered into the public sphere. Its presence expressed itself in a variety of ways. The Islamist "new women" who have made themselves visible over the issue of veiling, were situated mostly in the universities. The rising Islamist businessmen organised themselves in such associations as MÜSİAD (Independent Industrialists' and Businessmen's Association). New Islamic intellectuals have found an opportunity to spread their views to wider publics by way of large and small-scale press and media; in journals, newspapers and television. A new group of Islamically oriented engineers, physicians, governors and managers have succeeded in being appointed to high positions in state institutions, ministries, schools, and administrative post which had previously been closed to them.

It is, of course, impossible to analyse all these groups individually and in detail within the framework of this article, but I will try to make a general assessment. No doubt the *WP* consolidated and expanded its existence in the political domain thanks to the legitimacy and increasing strength in the legal, cultural, economic and social domains attained by the Islamic movement in the 80's. Both in terms of its social base of support and its political-cultural-economic program, this party is still in the process of defining itself. It represents a political-social movement in search of its own identity. This search for an identity is likely to continue for some time to come. In the words of a writer who closely follows the Islamic movements, this party has a political project and program which may be termed as "neither Shari'a nor democracy." On the other hand, as the same writer incisively observes, the WP is a party which negates, in quite an interesting way, the most important Islamist principle that religious affairs and state affairs cannot be separated from each other. In the WP, the leadership consists of either good orators, good organisers and/or good propagandists, but not of religious scholars. This fact, by itself, clearly demonstrates that in theory and in practice, the tendency within the WP is to make the religious authority subservient to the political one. There has been a gradual decline in the role of the ulema (religious scholars) and religious sects in the party. All of these developments show beyond doubt that the party has appropriated the most important institution of modernity, that is, the clear separation of religious affairs from state affairs. Consequently, we can conclude that, in essence, the WP is a political party wishing to obtain political power through political means. This conclusion validates the view that the WP's identity is but a secular identity wrapped in an Islamist garb.

The matter of Islamist women that has dominated Turkey's public agenda for some time, because of the issue of veiling, seems to contain a similar dual meaning. As researchers interested in the subject have rightly pointed out, the demand to wear Islamic dress which is the most visible expression of a collective demand for rights by Islamic women, does not fit traditional image of the Muslim woman. This new female (feminist?) Islamism is comprised of elite, urban, and well-educated university students. On the one hand, this movement presents itself in radical opposition to modernity. On the other hand, it also carries attributes of being a criticism, or even a refusal of traditional Islam. Moreover, the demands for the right to wear Islamic dress are voiced with reference to, or associated with reference to, or associated with, contemporary values such as individual freedoms, rather than Islamic references. It is also remarkable that the efforts to legitimise and rationalise different Islamic demands or challenges rely on the concepts, values and the discourse of modernity; that same modernity which the movement opposes.

The same is true for Islamist writers and intellectuals who have assumed the mission of disseminating and legitimising the Islamic worldview through newspapers, journals, books and private television stations. The most influential members of this group make an effort to express their world views with references

99

to the works of Western philosophers, writers and movements that reflect the spirit of the times. This, they do without neglecting to refer to the Islamic sources that proliferate in translation and that their readers have access to. In this context, during the last ten years, the western school of thought that has been most popular with this group was post-modernism and the famous writers and representatives associated with it. Post-modernism defends theses which postulate that cultures and civilisations are totalities closed to each other; that they could not be translated into each other; that universalistic, objectivist truth doctrines, epistemologies and world views such as enlightenment and positivism are out of fashion; that the great discourses are over; and that all stories or doctrines are equal in value. This kind of view constitutes the most valuable arsenal that Islamic intellectuals have hit upon in the last ten years. On the other hand, I must note that whether or not this cultural relativism is congruent with Islamic universalism and claims to possess the absolute truth is ignored with a telling postmodernist twist.

At this point, it will be useful to mention the structural changes that the old, traditional religious orders have gone through. In the traditional structure, the religious orders have acted as intermediaries between the individual and the state and kept a closed mürşit-mürit (spiritual teacher-disciple) relationship. As some observers have pointed out, recently, important changes have taken place because of the enormous changes and developments experienced in education and communication. Traditional face-to-face conversations in the religious orders have given way to mass meeting, conferences, television programs and videotapes. The accessibility of all texts and sources related to the subject, for the masses has strengthened the tendency to bypass the expert knowledge of mürşit or of the ulema. Perhaps the individualist, egalitarian tendency inherent in Islam which opposes hierarchical structures will come to fruition during this process under the conditions of the modern world. Or perhaps this process will make way for new forms of puritanism and expressions of personal piety, unparalelled until now in the history of Islamic piety.

It may be useful here to reflect on the phenomenon of a peculiar Islamic community leader, Fethullah Gülen. The teachings of Fethullah Hoca, as he is widely known, are actually part of the teachings of Nurculuk (a religious order) which recognises the full implications and requirements of modernity. His message appears to be a most peaceful and conciliatory project of harmony and integration for those segment of the population who feel they are being squeezed between the official modernisation program of the state and the need or desire to revive or live according to the traditional values of society. On the one hand such people do not want to reject outright the values brought about by modernity. Neither, do they want to turn their backs on the results of a tradition and cultural sensitivity that are over a thousand years old. For them, the thesis, or, in fact, the synthesis offered by Fethullah Hoca seems to provide a most admirable project.

Prospects for an Islamic democracy

The last fifteen years which will be associated with the name of Turgut Özal were very consequential for Turkey. Islamic fundamentalist developments which grew in that period deserve greater attention and more careful evaluation than they have gotten so far. It is not enough to summarily dismiss them as reactionary. This is not to deny that they suffer from severe deficiencies and inadequacies in terms of modern and democratic politics. There are hopeful signs in Turkey pertaining to the democratisation of Islam or the emergence of an Islamic version of democratic rule. However, we cannot ignore those developments that run counter to this trend and indeed threaten it. Democracy is new to Islam. The actors in the political and social arena lack the necessary familiarity with the subject. The traditional material that Islamic theory has at its disposal to cope with democracy is insufficient. This holds true even for the Islamic movements in Turkey which may be seen as the most experienced in democratic politics.

Ultimately, life will teach all the parties the lessons of modern life and social order. Indeed, this is partly what Fukuyama argues. In the theory that he developed based on Hegel, Fukuyama argued that all human beings are basically similar. Their basic needs and desires are comfort and ease in the physical domain, and prestige and recognition in the moral domain, and if in the moral domain the system satisfying the needs of prestige and recognition is democracy, than there is no reason for the people, the common people of Muslim societies; not to strive for these.

Finally, it is necessary to remember that it is not realistic to rely on the democratic interpretation of the theoretical-practical elements in the Islamic doctrine and traditions for the democratisation of Islamic countries. Modernity-and its important element democracy-did not spring in the West from within Christianity or because of a reinterpretation of Christianity from a democratic perspective. It arose largely despite Christianity, following certain developments. Christianity, its institutions and representatives, were forced to accept democracy in due time, after well-known bloody struggles. The same will be true for Islam. It is not very meaningful or practical to derive democracy from Islam. However, it is possible to Islamize democracy or to reconcile it with Islam. Islam, during its history, has appropriated many of the things, thought to be non- Islamic in the beginning. That is how it has secured its continued existence. Democracy has been powerful enough to demonstrate-and will continue to demonstrate in the future-that it is one of the most potent realities that Islam has the potential or the necessity to reconcile with.

Bibliography

Ahmet Aslan, "Demokrasiyi İslam'dan Çıkartmanın Yararı Yoktur" (No point in extracting Democracy from Islam), *Radikal,* 11 January 1997.

Ruşen Çakır, *Ne Şeriat Ne Demokrasi: Refah Partisini Anlamak,* (Neither Shari'a Nor Democracy, Understanding the Welfare Party) Metis Yayınları, İstanbul 1994.

Louis Gardet, *La Cite Musulmane, Vie Sociale et Politique,* Paris 1976.

Nilüfer Göle, "Urbaine, Instruite, Revendicative et Voilee", *Islamisme; les Dossiers de l'Etat du Monde,* Paris 1994.

Samuel Huntington, "Democracy's Third Wave", *Journal of Democracy,* Spring 1991.

Samuel Huntington, "The Clash of Civilisations?", *Foreign Affairs,* Summer 1993.

The Case of the Sudan, Papers presented at the Conference on the Situation of Human Rights in the Sudan, Turku/Abo 1997.

Ann Elizabeth Mayer, *Islam and Human rights,* Tradition and Politics, USA, 1991.

Ergun Özbudun, "Development of Democratic Government in Turkey: Crises, Interruptions and Reequilibrations", in *Perspectives on Democracy in Turkey,* Ankara 1988.

Elizabeth Özdalga, *Official Secularism and Popular Islam,* (Draft Paper), November 1995.

Association for Liberal Thinking
Freedom - Justice - Peace

Association for Liberal Thinking, established informally by a few like-minded people in December 1992, completed its official formation by April 1, 1994. The objectives of the Association as a non-profit, non-governmental organisation are to introduce the richness of the intellectual tradition that lay the heart of the liberal democratic civilisation to Turkish public; to engage in activities that promote understanding and acceptance of values like liberty, justice, peace, human rights, equality before law, tolerance, and to help development of acade-mic writing on liberal themes that will improve the ability of Turkish people to assess contemporary domestic and international changes; to attempt to find effective solutions to Turkey's problems within the classical liberal thought.

Association for Liberal Thinking does not involve in day to day politics and have no direct links with any political party or movement. Instead, as an independent intellectual grouping, it aims to set and influence broader political agenda so as to contribute to the liberalization of Turkey in economic and political fields.

Association for Liberal Thinking brings together talented and productive people whose belief in and commitment to liberty, free market economy, human rights and liberal democracy have been proved by their intellectual and professional work. It publishes books, journals; holds national and international symposiums; offers to non-official organisations educational programs on liberalism (its history, philosophical foundations and principal arguments) and other social theories like conservatism, socialism, social democracy as well as issues of contemporary social philosophy such as justice, liberty and human rights.

For more information please contact:

Özlem Çağlar-General Coordinator

GMK BulvanNo: 108/1706570 Maltepe Ankara, Turkey
Tel: 90.312. 2308703 Fax: 90.312.2308003

e-mail: liberal@ada.net.tr Web Site: www.//liberal-dt.org.tr

DATE DUE

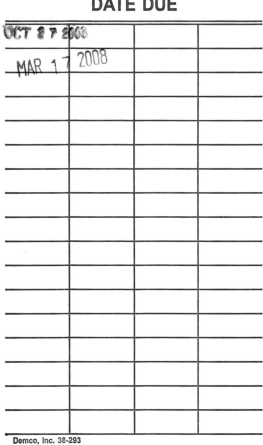

OCT 2 7 2005			
MAR 17 2008			